A New Life Awaits

Spirit Guided Insights to Support Global Awakening

Sheryl I. Glick RMT

RHG | MEDIA PRODUCTIONS™

A New Life Awaits:
Spirit Guided Insights to Support Global Awakening

Copyright © 2020 by Sheryl I. Glick

RHG Media Productions
25495 Southwick Drive #103
Hayward, CA 94544.

ISBN 978-0-578-63175-2 (paperback)

Visit us on line at www.RHG/MediaProductions or www.sherylglick.com

Printed in the United States of America.

Disclaimer

This book does not intend to offer specific medical suggestions, only opinion and heart felt awareness of certain universal problems. The views expressed are those of the author alone, and should not be taken as expert instruction or commands. The reader is responsible for his or her own actions. Adherence to all applicable laws and regulations, including international, federal, state, and local governing professional licensing, business practices, advertising, and all other aspects of doing business in the United States, Canada or any other jurisdiction is the sole responsibility of the purchaser or reader. Neither the author nor the publisher assumes any responsibility or liability whatsoever on the behalf of the purchaser or reader of these materials.

The information ideas and techniques in this book are not medical advice or treatment, but rather knowledge intended to assist the reader. It is the responsibility of the reader to seek treatment for any medical, mental, or emotional conditions that may warrant professional care.

Dedication

To my children, grandchildren, and their children.

To my friends and family, all part of a divine gift of life, a
blessed journey of love, renewal, rebirth, and evolution.

It is with gratitude to those in Spirit who have helped me into the world
to discover the meaning of loving myself and others and to finding
delight, joy, and happiness in the simple tasks of everyday living.

From world to worlds still unfolding, we travel our path to
self-awareness, we find it is only the energy of love and
compassion that connects, nurtures, and sustains us.

I thank all the forces of life and eternal life from the deepest
heartfelt connection we have created together and by
our shared experiences in this world and beyond.

Table of Contents

Acknowledgment

This book and all the people mentioned within the pages of this story, whether brought to me by varied coincidences or divine intervention, are now and forevermore intertwined within my heart and soul energy, joined to me, to be brought beyond this earth plane as part of my ever-expanding circle of family, friends, mentors, and soulmates. I thank each and every traveler through time and space who has shared their true measure of soul and physical life, bringing love and wisdom from above to this earth plane, illuminating our human hearts and spreading as much truth and hope into the world so life may be more meaningful and spectacular.

In conjunction with that thought, I would further like to thank each person whose stories appear boldly and honestly as accurately as I can remember them and as they actually happened. With gratitude for the time, energy, effort, and love each so freely gave in offering insightful lessons and intimate moments in the hope of helping me and others understand and improve their own challenges in life, I most humbly thank you.

For physically making it happen, much gratitude to my agent, Stacey Glick, Vice President of Dystel Goderich and Bourret Literary Management; also my daughter, who is a staunch supporter and a strong, sensible force for all things loving and good; RHG Media Productions; and many thanks to my family, both here in physical form and those in spirit who surround me and work with me in improving the quality of both my physical and soul experiences. They include; my assistant, Brooke Chamberlain; and family members; Hang Mui and Soso Mui and Henry Wong, my website and radio production managers; Deborah Beauvais, CEO of Dream Visions 7 Radio, which hosts my internet radio show, *Healing from Within*; as well as Brad Saul, CEO of Web Talk Radio, who has recently passed and was an encouraging energy force for my developing a level of proficiency in radio technique, and his helpful staff.

For intellectual stimulation and validation of my own inner thoughts and the development of my spiritual gifts, deep appreciation to the experienced authors, spiritual counselors, and medical doctors who have added much to my understanding of western and eastern medical disciplines and helped me express my hopes for us to incorporate the best of the many resources available to us for our personal care. Each person I have encountered has helped me enlarge the joy and happiness in my life, thereby allowing me to benefit from a more open mind and heart.

These include, in alphabetical order, Dr. Ruth Anderson; Sherianna Boyle; International Medium Robert Brown; Paul David,; Nancy Du Tertre; Paddy Fievet; Lorraine Flaherty; Barbara Furlani, R.M.T.; Carl Greer, Ph.D., Psy.D.; Marcia Garel, D.P.M .; Roberta Grimes, Esq.; Adam C. Hall; Carmen Harra, Ph.D.; Doug Heyes; Barbara Marx Hubbard; Brent N. Hunter; Nick Seneca Jangle ; Brian J. Katz, D.C.; Rev. Norbert Larcher; Eric Leuthardt, M.D.; Stephen Lewis; Gertrude Marks; Renee Messina, D.O .; Raymond Moody, M.D.; Lars Muhl; Master Ryoho Okawa; Michael Penchuk, D.P.M.; Don Miguel Ruiz, M.D.; Gary E. Schwartz, Ph.D .; Betsy Otter Thompson; Imre Vallyon ; Roseann Vanderbeck, O.T., Isabel Von Fallis; Alex Woodard; and so many more wonderfully open-hearted people. The people listed here have either been a guest on my radio show, *Healing From Within,* or work on a day-to-day basis in the search for understanding self on all levels and in service to making the world a healthier place.

For emotional latitude, many thanks to my family: my husband David M. Glick, Esq.; my daughter, Stacey; my son, Gregg, who has shared his story of healing and living well throughout the pages of this book; their spouses Jeremy and Lea; my grandchildren, Samantha, Alea, Chelsea, Talia, Sullivan, Greyson, and Graham; my sisters and their families; Margarita Barahona; and my family and guides in spirit, Mom and Dad, my sister, grandparents, aunts and uncles, much gratitude. They all have contributed to my developing a strong sense of the meaning of life.

I am especially thankful to my students and clients who have made a conscious effort to remove the layers and illusion of the stories they have created in their lives in search of their inner essence and soul power and to the countless others who find their way each day through the use of energy medicine, meditation, prayer, and open hearts to the truth and to the beauty of life eternal, too numerous to mention.

How thankful I am for the opportunity to experience life having my feet in two worlds, the physical and the spiritual. How much better life becomes when we are awakened to the true possibilities of our dynamic and ever-changing, eternal soul being.

Introduction

Many years ago, after a series of mystical experiences that I could not explain with my logical mind, I found myself experiencing feelings within that related to a life that was more than my physical experience. As I began to quiet my mind, I began to know my inner thoughts in a way that went beyond the five senses and the way I was accustomed to experiencing the physical world. I became aware that I was able to use an intuitive sense that had nothing to do with my mind, years of education, or life experiences. It was a sense of knowingness and awareness to history, our humanity, and the past in a way that went beyond normal explanation. In dreams and in my interactions with numerous people that I later discovered were Spiritual guides brought into my conscious reality for the important purpose of realizing my life plan and my inner soul being, a new awareness emerged, enabling me to constantly review past beliefs seen purely from a physical indoctrination of this time, place, and present life experience into another way. I am incredibly more able to accept new ways of knowing myself and those who walk this journey with me and to discern the true meaning of life.

When I had my first reading by a medium, Sonya Mitchell, over 20 years ago, I was told I would write three books, a trilogy. While I had no interest at that time in writing a book, much less three, Sonya seemed strongly convinced that this was a certainty. I kind of took her strange predictions with a grain of salt. But as one coincidence led to another person and event, over time I discovered that these happenings she had suggested were happening and were not random but orchestrated by a higher hand or some unknown force of life. We can begin to call this universal energy the divine source or God.

Years later, having completed my third book as directed by Spirit, apparently for the completion of my soul's promise to many people both in life and in Spirit, I see that it has unfolded this way.

My first book is *Life is No Coincidence: The Life and Afterlife Connection*, which shares my awakening process: going beyond my very practical, ego-minded reality to an awareness that we are indeed more than our body and are eternal beings connected to the Creative Force.

My second book, *The Living Spirit: Answers for Healing and Infinite Love*, shares stories of spiritual communication and my evolving ability to align to higher energy to channel Reiki energy and receive spiritual messages. *The Living Spirit* also reflects my transformation from merely a "being" of the physical world to my new perspective of the duality of life as energy beings or souls having a physical life.

I realize now the reason Spirit told me I had to do a third book, *A New Life Awaits: Spirit Guided Insights to Global Awakening*, about the new life we create each and every day of life by the choices we make and hopefully with a growing soul awareness of what waits for us beyond a short-lived physical life. We may learn about the journey of transcendence after physical death, hoping to ultimately prove our eternal soul meets all those loved ones in Spirit, where we continue on our journey of life for our continued personal soul development.

Whether in a body or in pure energy, the soul is the essence and complete oneness of Spirit's Intelligence and Universal Love and travels with us through time and space, lifetime after lifetime, as we gather experiences to refine our already magnificent soul. Death, in my opinion, is merely the next destination or adventure on our continuous circle of life.

There really is no death, only the unfolding of the infinite layers of realities that exist within us, in this world, and beyond. These layers are filled with the excitement and wonderment of the beauty of nature, friendship, memories, and experiences gathered during many lifetimes.

We must know that energy cannot be destroyed, so the energy of our thoughts and heart impulses must return to the place most people think of as Heaven, but is really simply the evolving expansion of creative life energy that is eternal. Whether in life or whether in Heaven, we are continually growing in our ability to gather love and compassion and to conquer any fear or darkness that might reside in our energy.

As a hospice volunteer, I have been privileged to serve end-of-life patients and their families by providing any assistance to make their transition to their new life as gentle and free of pain and fear as is humanly possible. Sometimes I was only meant to hold a person's hand or to listen to remembrances from their life stories or to hand them a glass of water.

Whatever interaction ensued, I tried to instill great trust in the final act of transcendence, knowing all was well and would be well as they journeyed beyond their physical body. None of us is ever alone, as we are surrounded by loved ones in Spirit, from the beginning of our life to the end, so know, therefore, death is just a new beginning.

A *New Life Awaits*, the title of this book, shares the truth known by many people who have felt that moment of complete awareness within them when this driving forceful energy, known as Spirit, awakens them and they learn decisively to love life, which is the ultimate gift from Spirit and which offers to each soul the chance for greater compassion for themselves and others. Of course, I didn't need to voice these understandings to these patients, for I hoped that my smile of reassurance would be enough to quiet fears about the unknown, often mysterious experiences they were going through.

I was trained not to voice my personal beliefs when sitting with patients. However, through my many life experiences and heightened soul energy, I could be telepathically sharing my beliefs from within the "soul-light force" that simply cannot be contained. This energy from Spirit or our interconnectedness to eternal life cannot be expressed easily in words. This energy might be represented by one's confidence or natural part of their physical, emotional, and spiritual presence. It cannot be forced or faked, and because it is authentic, it might help patients and their families feel less anxiety and fear about the dying process.

The stories you will encounter in this book that relate to my hospice experiences and encounters with many loving people may help you when you must deal with these issues in your own family life. All of us will face the loss of our loved ones, and we can do so courageously and with joy for a journey forward, embracing that process with a sense of grace and divine introspection.

In reading *A New Life Awaits*, I know you will discover much synchronicity with your own daily observations and find comfort in validating many of your dearest wishes to live life in an expansive and bolder approach, creating new perspectives, new thoughts, taking you in the direction that your soul and heart were born to experience. Unencumbered by the rules and limitations of societal or family systems that may have temporarily made you forget the amazing, loving, magnificent entity that you are that was born to walk in delight on our beautiful earth landscape and in spiritual light, you will find that a new life awaits you, and know you do not walk alone.

As spiritual beings having a human life experience, readers will also take away with them a greater awareness of human life in these tumultuous, changing modern times as we are encouraged to develop a more heightened and astute social consciousness in order to bring about worldwide cooperation when dealing with health, educational, medical, and political concerns affecting all of life: evolution in all our communities, spiritually and physically offering much needed new ways to go about eliminating injustice, the proliferation of crime, conquering disease, reinventing social graces and finding ways to integrate higher Universal Laws for wellbeing and success into our human daily lives. If we are being watched from above by those who live in gentler conditions than here on Earth and who, with love and hope for our advancement as a human species, expect us to expand and create more loving interactions and conquer warring impulses, the choice to do this is non-negotiable.

It is a big project to awaken and realize your true potential as a divine force for change and improvement personally and collectively, but it is also amazing to learn the truth. I hope within these pages you will find a new beginning for your own evolution.

CHAPTER 1
Life – The Gift of Universal Energy

When true self-remembering comes, one does not want
to alter oneself or others; one somehow rises above
their weakness and one's own. There can be no blame
anywhere. One swallows what is, and becomes free!
Rodney Collin, *Conscious Harmony*

The Day Begins

It is a bright promising day, but then each day that we awaken with the intention to send and receive the most positive thoughts and to have the greatest adventures, either for sheer fun or for learning about oneself, is a day when we all can remember to be grateful to be alive, conscious, and comfortable with our own energy, physical body, and spirit.

Each of us, I have discovered, has a specific unique destiny, experiences, and challenges that are included in a life plan or itinerary that comes into this world with us at conception. At conception, the soul part of life merges with physical body for the ultimate purpose of exploring our divine potential. I was reminded recently that true happiness can only be found by understanding our true worth as divine beings having a physical life. When we are able to discern our part in the process of creating happiness for ourselves and others, we will also recognize that the instinctual need to grow and put forth our presence in the world is really our reason for being.

Today unexpectedly a colleague in my office stood by my doorway and expressed to me that she was feeling stuck and was not giving enough to others and the world. I expressed to her that in having that thought, along with her deep sensitivity for living with kind intentions and her desire to give freely from her Inner Being, she was helping her soul expand and thereby improving the world. It is not in the "doing" but in the "becoming" that we honor the gift of life: learning, sharing, and exploring the many emotions that make us both human and divine. As we learn to feel through the sensory abilities of our body and differentiate the emotional thoughts of our mind, we evaluate repetitive situations, some fruitful and some less than productive, with greater efficacy. Our attention turns to adjusting our reactions and handling them in more successful ways. This only becomes possible as we begin to recognize childhood patterns that began with our initial experiences with trauma, sorrow, and sadness, often leading to loss of trust. As we mature, we search for ways to release these fears, often held at a deep cellular level, and to allow ourselves the leeway to rethink present-day behaviors and see old stories or memories in a more realistic way in order to develop creative means to bring about changes that enhance life. This process is happening to everyone, whether we are conscious of it or not. If we are truly honest with ourselves and move past denial, procrastination, and self-doubt, we begin to take responsibility for what needs to change in our thinking to allow ourselves to reach higher states of awareness.

It is quite possible we will discover the reason for venturing out of our original state of life: a spiritual, eternal world of Universal Energy and incarnate into this physical body, in a three-dimensional world. Many of the people I have encountered have suggested to me they would never have embarked on a physical life experience if they knew the pain and difficulties they would have to witness. But at the end of life, as a hospice volunteer, I have been happy to hear people on the brink of returning to their true form as soul beings express to me that life is good and beautiful.

As mentioned in my previous book, *The Living Spirit*, as an answer to this dilemma, I wrote, "Each of us is presented with a series of life experiences and lessons in order to learn and benefit our own soul awareness. In fact, we choose these experiences, pleasant or unpleasant, because of the lessons we need to have, which were chosen by us with the help of our teachers in spirit before we were born into this plane. Each life is important, and at the time of passing, regardless of how easy or hard life was, the soul values the opportunity it has had to increase its emotional quintessence. We have memories of whatever was meaningful and valuable to us and bring it along to the next stage of life.

It gave me great pleasure to interview Annie Kagan, an accomplished singer, composer, and chiropractor who wrote *The Afterlife of Billy Fingers*, on my internet radio show, *Healing from Within*, where she so beautifully and artistically expressed the value of every life, even those that another person may see as useless and wasted.

In our discussion, Annie used a term *"after-death communication,"* which is not to be confused with *"near-death experiences,"* as she described her confusion and initial doubt when a dialogue began between her and her brother, Billy soon after his passing. Annie, though she had developed a meditation practice says she is not a medium. However, it appears that clairaudience, using the gift of inner hearing, is the main way she was able to connect to her brother's spiritual energy. Her brother's mission, as he expressed to her, was to let her know the depth and tenor of his love for her and others he had harmed while alive, further explaining some events in his life, such as his addictions and behaviors that brought sadness to Annie and her family. "In later visits from Billy, he expressed the nature of life on earth as harsh and that is how it is supposed to be...not punishment for past transgressions, not about sin, either...but merely the way to remember the things we forgot from former times and places and to try to share our inner being, or soul energy, and love with others. It is a time for us to be seen and known."

Annie describes her joy in discovering how Billy in spirit finally found acceptance of himself. Though his life had been difficult, he still felt he had a great life. Now in the afterlife, he found "Divine Presence" in this new life and described it as "those beings in the atmosphere" who were wise, kind, super-evolved Beings whose loving custody he was in. Billy told Annie, "When you think about love with your human mind, you cannot fully access this over-the-top love you begin to feel for yourself and others: absolute acceptance without judgment, drama, or resistance."

It is my conclusion and was always my belief that everything in our life is exactly as it needs to be for us to have the experience our soul signed on for. Never doubt that you have everything you need to complete this wonderful journey of living, and do not be afraid to call on assistance from our friends above.

Returning to this universal sphere of continuous knowledge at that level of energy beyond this Earth, where the past, present, and future merge, Billy has shown us life goes on.

When I interviewed Annie, I had no idea that before long, my sister Rodelle would pass. As a medium, I received thoughtful, creative, validating messages for my clients. I assumed that was the way Spirit intended for me to use the gift of spiritual communication. However, I was told years ago that I could ask to speak to any soul energy, anywhere, alive or in spirit. I never tried to contact my own family members, as I felt that should they need to reach me, they would. Eight months after Rodelle's passing, I decided to meditate and try to check in to see how she was relating to her new world. Unlike Billy, who reached out to his sister, I reached out to mine in spirit.

Usually when I do a reading, I simply write down whatever is presented to me. It seems the information is usually perfectly tailored to what my client needs at the moment. With Rodelle, however, I decided to ask her questions. When she was ill, I tried so hard to show her that she was in for an amazing journey into forever and beyond, which was something Rodelle was not able to believe in. I already knew that there is no death, for our true-life essence, or soul, survives physical death. Sadly, she did not.

I soon felt her energy around me and sensed she was surrounded in a blanket of green glory and quietness, but her heart still hurt. She had not wanted to depart, as her love of life was quite palpable and her fight to stay alive was most courageous. I was aware that she was being cared for by souls and spiritual teachers that attended to her and her soul energy in the process of refreshing itself after her long, challenging illness and the sorrow of many personal disappointments in her past life. Healing of the soul is necessary before creating a new life in spirit filled with the effervescence and joy that many of us know or try to remember from our childhood of hope and possibility for love and friendship. My sister would fully heal with the help of the divine, as she was always one to try her best no matter what the challenge was.

I asked her who was there to meet her. Immediately I began to feel a pressure, a tightening on my head, as perhaps the drugs she was given before passing confused her. She was frightened. Our dad was calling to her to move forward.

Rodelle soon saw the head of the Statue of Liberty immense in size; the face was very close to her face. The beams of light from the crown on the statue's head enlarged, and many people moved forward to meet her: relatives, friends, and guides. Rodelle seemed to feel free, as the immigrants who had come to our shores looking for a new life must have felt, filled with the hope that they would be welcomed. Tears started to fill my eyes as I realized how joyful she was to find this new world and see so many souls she loved there to greet her.

Then I asked Rodelle if she was aware of how her daughters, granddaughter, and sisters were managing. She responded by showing pain, which I felt intensely in my left arm, and she expressed to me that relationships with several women in her life had been hard. Friends were easier for her to embrace than family members. It might be like that for all of us, since the family supplies the hardest challenges for resolving karmic cycles and some may not even be resolved in a single lifetime.

Quite suddenly, Rodelle's spirit and energy dancing around me seemed to lift up, and she expressed that since there were many old thoughts still within her, opening the door to the exquisiteness of this new vision of light and energy was taking some time. I saw in my inner vision an astronaut floating in space trying to move freely and easily without gravity holding him back, but wearing the spacesuit was still a hold to life that had to be discarded for Rodelle to be truly free. Moving past that impression, I sensed a playful and joyful picture, like the new paintings Rodelle had purchased before her passing, which included a collage of a dog's face with bright colors. She had so loved her dog, Oliver.

The next impression I received was a man sitting in a chair reading a book experiencing heavy sinus pain, maybe allergies or emotions tied to events that couldn't be changed. Unaware of who that person was, I can only surmise it was her husband. Next, I saw an Indian man in a canoe paddling very fast, wanting to get home, but was still far away, and I sensed the words, "Only time changes things." I heard the name Hiawatha. Later upon goggling that name, I discovered Hiawatha's wife, Minnehaha, had died before he did. Maybe Rodelle was showing me her husband was not ready to meet her yet and had more time. Though years older than she was, four years after her passing, he is still living.

I then asked Rodelle if she saw her new great-grandson, Dylan, who had recently been born, and she responded by showing me she was as proud as a rooster flapping its wings and was "kvelling," as the old Jewish expression goes.

The final message shared with me showed me conclusively that she had found a new soul family in spirit and was helping others, as it was the best way she had discovered to serve. *How beautiful,* I thought, and knew that she was safe.

For some time after this reading with Rodelle, I often loved to think of my sister as being surrounded and loved in the blanket of green glory and quietness, as it was soothing to me and helped me resolve the sorrow of her difficult illness and passing.

Then, I believe, I was given a great gift from Spirit when I received in the mail a small but extremely powerful book by Lars Muhl entitled *The Gate of Light* and invited Lars to be a guest on *Healing From Within.* The book offered a spiritual practice created over 2500 years ago by the Essene mystery school, which Jesus, Mary, and Joseph were connected to. There were many synchronistic explanations for me in this book, but one that immediately made me cry is related in the following passage written by Lars Muhl: "The intelligence of the heart works on a completely different frequency from that of the brain. Whereas the intelligence of the brain is connected to the electrical system of the body, the intelligence of the heart connects with the Heavenly Essence and the Plane of Unity, God. The practice of Thankfulness can be carried out only through contact with the Heavenly Essence. This contact, once established, alters the electrical system at the level of the individual cell. Through neutrinos, which possess the ability to break through all physical states, light from the Heavenly Essence is spread throughout the body, including all the etheric and astral layers. Each one of the body's cells possesses a receptive factor, which, if open and active, is able to receive information from other cells. After this process, through the tireless struggle of an individual, reaches its full maturity, the final stage of awareness and transfiguration presents itself at some point. This is what happened to Yeshua on the Mount of

Transfiguration when, clothed in *His Robe of Glory, a fully enlightened person, He showed mankind the bliss that awaits the patient practitioner.*"

When reading these same words in Lars's book *The Gate of Light* that I had heard in my reading with Rodelle, I believed my sister in spirit had been shown the loving kindness and healing from Jesus and was able to explore her new life and world with pristine joy.

❖

Therefore, it seems in one way or another, we are being given messages to elevate our hearts. As we tap into our intuition supported by meditation practices, we can strengthen personal resolve or resilience. Resilience is a great force, in my estimation, for spiritual growth. Recently I found an article in *Time Magazine*, the June 1, 2015 edition, in the section "Frontier of Medicine" and read "Bounce Back," written by Dr. Dennis Charney Dean, Icahn School of Medicine, who wrote, "For resilience there's not one prescription that works. Find what works for you." As a psychiatrist, Dr. Charney knows there are many benefits to moving beyond your comfort zone for the development of resilience, which he says is a set of necessary skills. Compelling new research about resilience also is now focusing on "the state of mindfulness" that we are hearing so much about, as today's culture is consumed with seeking a greater awareness of Self, energy, and a means to improve health and longevity. Mindfulness can be considered to be a state of conditioning or training in order to stay focused in the moment on the activity or event being engaged in rather than allowing the mind to wander and think about other distracting influences.

Surprisingly after reading that article about resilience and mindfulness as necessary tenets for the development of one's state of well-being and happiness, my husband, David, an attorney, nonchalantly handed me an article from *The New York Times* newspaper on May 14, 2015, entitled, "Public Defender Beats Partner on Happiness Scale for Lawyers." The article states that of the rewards associated with becoming a lawyer—wealth, status, and stimulating work—day-to-day happiness has never been high on the list and further suggests that lawyers and law students may be focusing on the wrong rewards. It was noted that public defenders or Legal Aid attorneys were more likely to report being happy than those lawyers in high-income or partner-track jobs at prestigious law firms. This article merely served to reinforce my own intuitive feelings that the values and dreams from earlier times, cultures, and societies have been reinvented with less moral intent, much like the political, economic, and social conflicts being addressed in the 2016 presidential election.

The American people are ardently demanding changes to present corrupt, political, elitist, ruling-class practices that do not allow simple, kind, good values to be honored. As we question what we want in life and what is truly a just criteria for success, we are discovering that people embroiled in only a materialistic approach to life—either forgetting or never having considered their equally important spiritual needs for love, for compassion, to be of service to others, and to be free from greed— have become disconnected and dissatisfied. The quote by Shakespeare's Polonius, "[t]o thine own self be true/And it must follow, as the night the day/Thou cannot then be false to any man," is still a rightful way to approach and remember our deepest personal needs as well as the reason we incarnated into this life.

I have observed people who are not only happy and fulfilled, but often courageous and dynamic and bold leaders much needed in today's world of conflict and confusion. Their general mindset reflects virtues including empathy, the acceptance of others with genuine regard for their differences, and respect for what we all can contribute to the world.

In other words, these successful people are the antithesis to the competitive, unrelenting, and controlling drives of many of our politicians, corporate leaders, educators, and media who display a dog-eat-dog mentality.

Recently, in listening to the news about the presidential candidates, I have been drawn into the problematic drama and find it unsettling. As an empath, I deeply feel the anger of some of the American people, which is so untypical of many of the people of our nation. I find it difficult to understand how leaders who have been given the best in life in the way of education, home, and innate intelligence and have chosen a life in public service have forgotten their good fortune, moving away from the true virtues of Spirit.

Discussing this with a fellow worker at my office the other day, I suggested that the 2016 election seemed to be a battle between the old and the new, perhaps good and evil. This was on my mind as I left work on Saturday afternoon and headed to the movies to see *Independence Day*.

July 4th was approaching, and I was hoping to rid myself of the sadness I was feeling that was fueled by many recent world events. I most definitely look to be inspired. Standing in front of me in the ticket line was a woman who turned around and asked me what movie I was going to see. She then said, "I am Christian, and they often have Christian movies here." I told her I saw such a movie not long ago, *Miracles from Heaven*, about a little girl who was dying, had a near-death experience, and then heard God tell her she must go back. Her doctors found her to be healed, a true story and a true miracle. "Miracles happen more often than most people know," I told her. I paid for my ticket, said good-bye, and went to buy popcorn. I sat down to wait, as there was some time until the movie started. As I turned to my left, I saw the same woman sitting cross-legged on the bench. I asked her what movie she had decided to see and she said, "None." Surprised by her answer, I started to talk to her, and she told me that each day, she read a portion of the Bible and then prayed. Her family was Catholic, but she was more in favor of a personal communication with God and was finding it to be her way. I mentioned that I had discovered through my hands-on healing work and meditation a loving connection to Spirit and knew things that no book or person could explain or teach me. True growth often comes from personal experience. Then I told her what a hard time I was having, watching all the killing and violence in the Middle East and seeing a world implode in anger and lack of humanity. She looked directly into my eyes and said, "It has never been different. There will always be strife, but we must trust and allow God to work in his way. Whoever becomes president will be the right one for now and give us the experience the world needs." Funny, I thought, but how often I had said the same exact words to others? And now it seemed I needed to hear it from someone else. I knew God was asking me to trust and surrender to His plan and not to worry. I rose to go to the theatre, turning back for a moment to ask her name. "Rebekah," she responded, and then we went in different directions.

❖

As a child, like many other spiritually sensitive children, I frequently experienced fear at bedtime, as often there was an uncomfortable presence in my room. Each night I fled my bedroom, creeping along the dark hallway to find my parents' bedroom, where I hoped I would be protected. My parents did not understand—as many parents, even today, when there is great discourse on the needs of sensitive children, still, they do not completely understand—the influence that energy has on our physical and emotional wellbeing. When any person lets you know they are physically uncomfortable by a dream, a person, or a place, it must be taken seriously, not laughed or joked about. Nor should they be told that they are just too sensitive or imagining things. It is a great gift to feel the nuances of energy, life forms, and a higher sense of self and should be encouraged.

My question as an adult became, "Where must we begin to encourage the changes needed to help develop mentally, physically, and spiritually strong children and adults as well as healthy, communities that are educationally sound and thriving economically and artistically?" Perhaps we must begin with our perceptions and a look at our physical and spiritual realities. It goes back to our present-day views of what is important to us materially and spiritually and how society either values or devalues basic human decency. Everywhere we are assigned designations or labels: boy or girl, rich or poor, beautiful or ugly, smart or unintelligent. I feel labeling a situation or a person in this way—or with either an illness or a mental or social disorder other than to help them receive the services they need—might be detrimental. Labeling will set them on a path that is unalterable and will allow fewer opportunities.

Our physical life, mind, and ego are obsessed and defined by labels and descriptions of who we think we are based on the perceptions of others, and buying into this thinking makes us forget our inner soul presence and needs. At no time in my life have I heard more negativity, name-calling, and labeling than in the 2016 Presidential Election campaign. I was quite amazed by people who had achieved so much but who had declined in spiritual values, as evidenced in the way they handled policy and communication of their views about the important plans for the country. Several candidates, party members, and the media wasted so much time and energy on accentuating personality flaws and attacking past indiscretions. But perhaps the stakes were huge. Corruption and mismanagement of the government by many misguided politicians were now even more overwhelming apparent, so a new leader dedicated to restoring the nation to life, liberty, and the pursuit of happiness for all needed to be chosen. We needed a new vision and a tough leader to address the many problems our nation and world faced.

The themes and the many problems that plagued the 2016 Presidential Election included: people living in war-zone-like neighborhoods plagued with drug issues, alcoholism, poverty, homelessness, decline of the family, immigration issues, welfare dependency, teenage pregnancies, diseases, and multiple other health issues. Our society and the many institutions designed to correct these problems by providing programs for self-improvement, hoping to assist individuals to secure better-paying jobs for a more prosperous life, have not been effective nor provided enough positive results from these efforts. Clearly new efforts were needed.

While I was on my July 4, 2016, vacation to Maine, the nation was able to see unconscionable happenings, all symptomatic of a world on fire and preferential treatment for certain people that has gone on far too long, unchallenged and unresolved by our world leaders, including our American government. In early July, we all watched as the FBI director, at a press conference, explained why he was making the decision that the presidential candidate who had handled confidential documents while performing the duties of Secretary of State without proper security was, in his opinion, not susceptible to further investigation or consequences. Hearing him describe her indiscretions and then saying he saw no grounds for going further with an indictment sounded clearly counterproductive. The people standing next to me in the lobby of the hotel all gasped in astonishment at his decision. Years later, the country would still be divided as a result of the lack of justice perceived by the public in that moment of this unprecedented and confusing announcement. Many people sensed that an elected official was allowed to receive a free pass in the face of credible evidence and also witnessed her extreme contempt for the process of law by destroying e-mails and electronic data requested by the authorities. Implementing new laws that hold "anyone" and "everyone" accountable for unlawful acts regardless of privilege or political status must be demanded. Dissatisfaction with the government's handling of sensitive events like this and the lack of equality observed, both economically and socially, have led to violence, lawlessness, and the lack of trust in our politicians and elected officials. An investigation by Congress into what actually happened in the 2016 election where a Russian collusion or involvement theory was suggested is still going on. We can only hope people who acted incorrectly will be held accountable.

We simply must listen to the needs of each group of people and make serious efforts to bring about family conditions, work initiatives, and government policies that actually work. We have to repudiate this unfounded belief that we can do whatever we want without regard for personal and societal consequences. This belief that we can do whatever we want has become a mantra for our free society and the politically correct culture that has taken hold in our nation, but in reality, of course, we cannot do whatever we want without consequences. We cannot do what is only good for one segment of our country but must respect and help all groups without favoring one group over another, which ultimately brings about lawlessness and violence. Wherever there is injustice, there will always be those people who seek justice and truth and who will stand up honestly and voice their concerns, hopefully without the use of violence, but instead offering fair solutions and then implementing them.

Now, we are entering a time of great personal spiritual awareness, and there is more than disappointment when people do the wrong things repeatedly. I am reminded of the protests I witnessed in the 1960s, when Martin Luther King led African Americans to seek greater equality, but wisely, as he did it peacefully, gracefully, artfully, and honestly. As a result of his work, the African American groups have improved their conditions immensely, as can be seen by their success and integration in every area of work, art, sports, and all professions in the country. Much progress has led to more people living better. There still is a great deal of work in supporting minority groups living in substandard conditions in inner cities here and in the world. The work begins with our realization that political groups have not fulfilled their promises to most minorities. Filling top leadership positions with those who truly wish to serve honestly and who will not be consumed by the lobbyists and interests that try to buy their votes and allegiance should be happening now. Only people who have evolved to a level of appreciation for their own success and joy in life and who wish to serve for the highest good of *all* can be the best leaders in these changing times, as our citizens spiritually awaken to their multidimensional status and their many new human capabilities.

❖

The focus has too long been simple "happiness." Some people will do anything to ensure their own happiness. Happiness is however, the result of a purposeful life and a realization of our human and spiritual qualities.

Chaney Weiner, author of *Because This is Your Life*, writes, "You are here to do amazing things in your life because you are a special person who has something of tremendous value to contribute to the world that is based on what is most important to you...Do what inspires you most; don't let other people be a dark cloud that stops you from realizing the glowing truth that's responsible in uncovering the magnificence of who you are; and don't give up, don't ever give up."

We have spoken of educational and political realities making it clear to us that major changes are long overdue in our world. Quantum physics has made clear to the scientific community that everything is energy and all energy is interconnected, so we are part of a divine matrix of Energy, God or Source, and the force for creation and continuous expansion. We are indeed evolving and are at a crossroads for human and divine potential to expand and for solving many of the problems we have been discussing.

These worldwide evolutionary patterns are profoundly changing at this time. It is no longer possible to shunt aside or deny what is really happening, and people will stand up to assist others in protests, marches, and gatherings to help us move towards this divine right to happiness and success. Many of us are becoming intensely aware as we flock to develop multiple practices—including energy-healing work, yoga, meditation, and a return to nature—that what we are really seeking is a connection to our original state of divinity, not from the place a material lifestyle and thoughts of 'more and more' have taken us.

*Remember: even the challenges, no matter how
hard, must be experienced in order to understand the
strength and power of our divine energetic being.
It is this consciousness or remembrance of self
that is the way for self-improvement.*

In conjunction with this growing awareness of our soul divinity, Spirit guides us to meet people in our daily life whom we may simply enjoy knowing or whom we may learn something from. It doesn't have to be monumental, either. I recently decided to change beauty salons, returning to a place I had been the year before, looking for a new colorist. I asked the woman who was blowing out my hair to point out the colorists to see if I could recognize the person I had talked to when I had been in the shop a year earlier. I was shown four different people and recognized Yanice. It was like seeing a long-lost friend. Success at last! As Yanice was working on me, I mentioned that I was an intuitive healer and medium, and she asked, "What is your name?" I said "Sheryl." She lit up with excitement and said, "I know you! I have your book. I got it at my chiropractor's office in the waiting room, and I borrowed it to read." Yanice went over to everybody in the shop and said, "Look, there are no coincidences! And nothing is random. We do meet the people that we are supposed to meet at the right time."

In the past several years, I have noticed through my own personal connections with family, friends, and clients that as we ride through life, much like the joyful merry-go-round ride of our childhood, we experience much joy, terror, or even a combination of both. Reminded of experiences from our earlier life, we approach rapidly changing times with the same simplicity of earlier training, which, although correct, may not be sufficient to deal with the challenges of our adult life. Still these old-fashioned values of our youth are the foundation of our humanity. It is therefore a great sadness to those of us born in a different era to see values such as love of country being dishonored by unhappy youths who burn our flag and denigrate our passion for freedom. To witness anything less than living honorably with these well-relied-on ethics is not an option, as we have discovered the real goal of life is to become or remain righteous citizens.

Remember your childhood as I remember mine! The best hopes for happiness come from the best memories and happiness experienced in childhood and a trust in a timeless, universal plan.

When I was a child, each night I repeated this small prayer. No one taught it to me, but still I knew it. It went like this:

Lord keep us safe this night
Secure from all our fears.
May angels guard us while we sleep
Till morning light appears
Amen.
- John Leland

In a recent interview, Garnet Schulhauser, author of *Dancing Forever with Spirit*, expressed his feeling that every child begins at an early age, to know that all humans have a soul. He wrote, in regard to dealing with any bullying situation, "The best way to stop bullying begins at home. Parents should strive to avoid negative responses to events and demonstrate to their children that it is important to show love, compassion, and forgiveness to all other people. Children should be taught at an early age that all humans have souls and that all souls are connected to the Source and to one another. They should be encouraged to listen for messages from their guides and helpers in Spirit and not allow negative emotions or fear to rule the day."

Like Garnet, who values the voice of Spirit and soul and sharing this with all our children, we might observe that only recently, Pope Francis arrived in New York City, sharing his words, actions, and hopes for raising the values of mankind to the original message from his ancient religion, Catholicism, and to Jesus's messages of encouragement for the betterment of humanity and the God they both hold so dear.

Pope Francis's moral sensitivities defy standard public sentiment, going beyond the limitations of his traditional religious training and to authentically represent a personal connection, unity, and goodness with all human beings of any religious persuasion and to be one with God. Pope Francis speaks from his mind and heart, rides on buses, and hangs out with the poor. In my humble view, his openness and expansive spiritual understanding of the Universal Laws of Spirit and God are a vision as well as an approach to inspire other worldwide patriarchal religions and their followers, so we may all come together in a meeting of Oneness and a love for God, humanity, and nature. This belief might essentially be a message that our political leaders can embrace in order to engage in a new, trustworthy way. Getting it right now during this crucial shift in world, political, and religious divisiveness is becoming increasingly critical.

> *Pope Francis in his open hearted expressions of goodness and wisdom represents Spirit infused in his humanity, sharing a divine soul presence as well as love for life, with expansive expressions of humility, honor, integrity, and a true regard for the spark of the Divine residing in each of us, which when found, is known to be love.*

CHAPTER 2
Death Be Not Proud

Death be not proud, though some have called thee...
Die not, poor Death, nor yet canst thou kill me...And
death shall be no more; Death, thou shalt die.
John Donne

Recently, I interviewed Luke Adler, author of *Born to Heal*. Luke is an intuitive healer and spiritual teacher practicing Chinese Medicine and other ancient modalities. In relation to an understanding of life and death, Luke wrote, "One of my mentors shared with me that people build their lives around avoiding three things: loss, anxiety, and death. The only problem is that loss, anxiety, and death are the three things you are guaranteed to face in life."

Death, one of Luke's references and the fear that most people focus too much attention on, was never an overwhelming concern of mine. Even though my family members spoke in quiet whispers whenever the subject surfaced, in hindsight, I remember vividly that in seventh grade, the boy who sat next to me in science class didn't appear one morning. He was never absent, and I wondered where he was. Later on, I was told by another student that he had died in an accident. I knew somehow, he was still nearby and still the same delightfully mischievous fellow I knew. I don't know why I didn't feel the end of my connection to him, but of course, at that time, I was not aware that in the deep, hidden recesses of my subconscious mind, the truth lay dormant waiting to be proven to me: "There was no death, only a return to life beyond here." However, if dying is a concern of yours, I hope that what you read in the following pages of this book will allow you to remember that part of yourself, that soul essence, which may have gone unexamined for some time or may have been damaged or tarnished by the well-meaning people around you who may also have forgotten their true divine essence. It is my hope that you may retrieve a 'knowingness' of your soul essence that experiences peace, love, compassion, and a fluid movement through time and space eternally, allowing you to enjoy both a physical life today and "existence" beyond this physical life tomorrow. What you may well discover if you keep an open mind is how to live vibrantly in the two realms of life: the physical and the spiritual.

Minister Rev. Keiko Hoshino, is a representative from Happy Science, a spiritual foundation founded by Master Ryuho Okawa. Because of Master Okawa's new book, *Miraculous Ways to Conquer Cancer*, she was a guest on my show, sharing how Master Okawa realistically shows the way we can establish how we might live when we pass from this time and place to Spirit. Master Okawa suggests, and I feel this to be appropriate, that when we live life in a bold, creative, and interactive way with people and our planet, the life we will establish beyond here will be reflective of this proactive lifestyle. It seems that it is worth our while to expand our spiritual awareness, if for no other reason than that we want a great Afterlife experience.

Master Okawa wrote, "The physical body which is visible is not the only factor that makes up a human being. We actually have a spiritual body that dwells in our physical body: and this spiritual existence has a multi-layered structure where the outer layer is called the astral body and is shaped in similar fashion to the human body. It is this energetic body that survives physical death." Master Okawa goes on to suggest that sometimes the pain from illness and disease is taken back to the other world and the soul has difficulty releasing it. "For example, the person who has not awakened to their true nature as a human being with a spiritual existence is not fully aware of how he is meant to live in the world after death."

If you choose to have the best life after this one, awakening and evolving now is a very good reason to take your spiritual growth seriously and to resolve karma or negative issues now."

It seems we must do the work now if we are to reap the rewards later.
We are apparently creating our next version of life by how much
effort we put into awakening to our spiritual constitution.

Though I was saddened, even as a child, to see how many people live their lives and adhere to belief systems that appear to have many inaccuracies or omissions from the truth, as noted in religious, economic, political, medical, and educational philosophies and practices, either purposefully or unknowingly, many leaders seek to control the resources of their groups, often using mind-control techniques to empower certain people while disempowering others. It may be these restrictions to developing the fullness of our human and spiritual capacity for love and fluidity in creating our best life that we must overcome, so that we may eventually prosper in our afterlife.

Marie D. Jones, author of *Mind Wars*, offers a very comprehensive understanding of the subversive alteration and modification of human behavior. Marie writes, "The mind to us, is ours and ours alone, and even our closest loved ones only get to know what we chose to share with them.... Our minds are our minds. Yet from the beginning of time, others have desired to make us think, believe, and behave according to *their* minds, and the desire to control the most private and powerful part of our identity was a golden fleece, a Holy Grail, to those whom, for whatever motive or purpose, would benefit from being the puppet master to our puppet. Mind control is probably as old as our awareness that we each had a mind of our own."

Our minds may be subject to brainwashing, coercion, manipulation, or psychological programming, but the soul, the true essence of our being, is not subject to anyone's control or direction. When in alignment to the universal source of life, you have the truth and can always respond with goodness and a true rendering of what is best for yourself and others.

Your personal power is yours alone to hold and
can only be taken away if you allow it.

All beautiful souls must strive to find ways to move beyond the manipulation and mind control perpetrated by society and our earlier upbringing in order to discover that we are not alone, and that loved ones on both sides of life, our earth life and our eternal life, surround us with their courageous hopes and whispers of life and afterlife possibilities. You don't even necessarily need an illness or insurmountable challenge to tap into this place of uncompromised support for your soul and mind truth. You might have a dream, hear a song, take a walk along a mountain trail or an ocean shore, or eat a divine meal and in a moment of joy, realize that you have everything you need within yourself to live fearlessly and to conquer this illusion of mind control and death. In that moment, you are free to explore your inner landscape and to visualize what it is you truly long for.

In recent days, I have seen so many people in their hearts and minds being adversely affected by cancer. It seems we have reached epidemic proportions alongside other seriously challenging ailments attributed to an aging population and the stresses of modern-day life. Many have forgotten what our religious institutions have always held dear, the fact that the soul is an energy force of eternal magnitude and that a new life awaits us beyond illness, beyond fear, beyond sorrow or pain. But the focus while living must be to live with joy, hope, and a full appreciation for the beauty and value of life. Sometimes a disease or tragedy or changes in the world condition may help us reconnect to our eternal truths and further our soul as well as our physical life growth.

As I observe this continuous chain of friction among people, nations, and our major institutions, within families, and observe increasing numbers of natural disasters; war; genocide; terrorists; people waging war with themselves and succumbing to addiction, alcoholism, drugs, and other self-defeating illnesses; and people who simply feel disempowered, overwhelmed, and unable to participate in living their daily lives with vitality, I like to remember that these seemingly disheartening events are simply the means to begin to know the many layers and dimensions of self, life, and change and are efforts to move us from pain to pleasure and eventually our spiritual afterlife.

Changing attitudes and perceptions to embrace a higher awareness of eternal nature allows us to shift to working cooperatively for the good of all, improving life now and later.

Call me a dreamer, but if we need to go to a dream state in order to realize who we are and what we are capable of achieving, if we need to move past the social mores and painful interactions of our earlier experiences, then I will call you to join me in this dream state. In hindsight, I remember my childhood and my parents and the other adults in my early life who were products of the Great Depression and World War II and know that what I witnessed then, and what I felt emanating from their energy trails, was anxiety and fear for the survival of their families. They worked hard to provide the necessities of life-sustaining needs, shelter, food, clothing, and medical care, as we still do in these times. Yet, in those days, I also remember much lightness, joy, happiness, and their bright hopes and efforts to see that their children would be spared the hardships they experienced. There was love and gratitude for what they *did* have. Not being as overwhelmed by the media, internet, and all other technological sources as we are today and which may be taking us away from more satisfying social interactions, those in the past had more time to reflect and connect to Spiritual energies. This time helped nurture their family life, which, in turn, nourished the baby-boomer generation, many of whom went on to have expansive and successful lives, surpassing their parents by securing advancements in education, family, home, travel, and financial security and living the American dream. We have moved away from these gentler values and are presently observing many disturbances to our mental, physical, societal, and spiritual health. This unnatural involvement with social media is sure to promote more compulsive and undesirable mental states, and it may be said one day that the path of past generations was remarkably less challenging in many ways than our more advanced, technologically savvy modern world, where so much communication is merely between people and machines.

While technology is necessary, it must be used reverently and simply as a tool, or it will ultimately change the way people interact with each other, the planet, and Universe. Research on happiness, health, and well-being shows us that maintaining social interaction and relationships is still the key in creating and sustaining a happier and healthier population. When people are less involved in socialization processes and are limited from speaking one-on-one, face-to-face, they lose the ability to understand body language and to gain more information from the actual physical reactions that come from this type of interaction. Text messages and e-mails are being overused and seem to be dehumanizing and affecting our capacity to feel, empathize, and communicate with skill, which aids in receiving pleasurable responses. I fear for our next generation, the children and leaders of tomorrow.

Dr. Larry Rosen, a previous guest on my radio show and author of *iDisorder*, is also most concerned about the long-term effects of social media on our population and how it will affect either introverts or extroverts. Dr. Rosen writes, "Researchers have begun to identify certain personality traits that lead to an increased chance of becoming an addict and one trait that is quite common is known as 'Harm Avoidance.' Some characteristics shared by people with this tendency are: they often prefer to go out of their way to avoid uncomfortable situations, and they are low in reward dependence or not receiving pleasing stimuli from their environment and therefore respond to the internet better since often their responsiveness to verbal approval and social reinforcement is low. They also seem to have little tolerance for unpredictable frustrations in their life and avoid confrontation at all costs. They may also exhibit symptoms of depression, and according to The *National Institute of Mental Health*, nearly 1 in 5 adults will suffer from some form of depression in their lives."

For those who study history and human nature, we know that in every time period, people and cultures have had challenges, and yet, the world continued no matter what. Today, issues of global warming as well as environmental issues concerning drinkable water, enough food to feed the masses, and the depletion of many resources lead us to wonder how we will sustain the massive world population. New diseases appearing and old diseases resurfacing, the decline of the family structure, too many self-absorbed people, materialistic consumption depleting our world resources at an alarming rate, and the advancement of technology concern me. It would be advantageous to all if leaders of corporate America, our politicians and government officials, and lobbying groups began to look beyond their immediate goals for monetary compensation and see life ahead as it will be without the necessary changes or precautions that are needed at this time. We may look at the resurging protests and violence in minority neighbors and the loss of respect for our police and military that have been allowed by groups that have agendas for a few, not for all.

Many pressing issues need to be rethought and improved. The Federal Drug Administration and its policies have limited the approval of certain alternative healing approaches, which might work alongside traditional cancer treatments. I read only the other day that forty percent of medical students are entering the field of oncology, as it is lucrative and we have an epidemic of cancer. I would hope the drive to heal people would be as important to the doctors as the money they hope to receive. Seems we are truly at a crossroads of human and spiritual divisiveness and the Universe is witnessing humanity face an increased assault by a world threatened by its own actions.

The Universe, it appears, is asking us to pay attention, wake up, and go beyond all differences and limited thinking to observe, make corrections, and reevaluate priorities and values. Let's help the coming generations to have multiple and plentiful opportunities to live and discover the beauty and awe-inspiring hopes of past ancestors who were able to forgo uncontrolled impulses for material gains alone, finding genuine or authentic human qualities. I grew up in a time when there were peace movements along with world concerns for idealistic approaches to living well and where personal fulfillment was a valued commodity. But always, we brought the precious values of our ancestors in spirit with us, which positively affected our decision-making process and added to our spiritual awakening. Now, we must continue to work with all aspects of our physical and spiritual lives, to heal and create a world that offers hope in the face of personal or collective hardships, that may make us forget our divinity and ability to live with dignity. If we begin to do what feels right from within, without judging issues as good or bad, only as experiences, we will free ourselves from the many illusions or ideologies that still hold us prisoners to fear and the limitations of our conditioned minds and lift these challenging times to new heights for advanced human evolution.

Out beyond ideas of wrongdoing and right doing
there is a field. I'll meet you there.
When the soul lies down in that grass the world is too full to talk about."
-Rumi

In recognizing your divinity, you will begin to hear your inner voice. The inner voice is the way to the soul and proof that the soul and your memories are eternal. Before awakening to thoughts of your inner soul voice and its eventual announcement that we all survive physical death—therefore, consciousness survives physical death—we cannot know this voice is of Spirit. This voice is the whisper of guidance from a Higher Self, a gut feeling connected to the mind and also the innate cellular intelligence of Creation. If you realize you are surrounded by the guidance of a Universal life force, everything is possible. However, if you cannot access your inner voice fear and ego-based illusions will allow a constant flow of mind chatter. Mind chatter merely limits you from truly connecting your heart's soul-based truth with your mind and holds you back from healing, loving, and living life with joy.

CHAPTER 3
Coincidences, Synchronicities and Miracles

We hold these truths to be self-evident, that all men are created equal,
that they are endowed by their Creator with certain unalienable Rights,
that among these are Life, Liberty and the pursuit of Happiness.
Declaration of Independence, July 4, 1776

By observing a host of coincidences, synchronicities, and miracles and simply listening and talking to everyone I meet, I have become aware that Spirit brings new people to us constantly who seem challenged by their experiences, and this has led me to seek an explanation of why souls who live in a dimension of eternal oneness and unity would chose to come into the physical world. **In this physical world, where first, as children, they would forget who they were and then struggle through confusing, sometimes frightening, or even painful childhood experiences only, if they are paying attention and lucky, to discover the means necessary to establish conditions that allow their soul to weather any storm and survive in a more courageous way so some might eventually become leaders, lovers, providers, healers, or simply observers of life.** It could be that the loss of childhood innocence is the prerequisite Spirit imposes on us so we may create the necessary circumstances for recognizing any limitation and then moving past it.

These mystical observances, as well as the ordinary experiences of daily life, are part of the fiber of our energetic life and of All that is for all time.

Yesterday while at Costco, a gigantic discount superstore, I was eating lunch, and a young college student and her mom sat down next to me. I heard the student express how some people made so much money, and others, who had more skills, might not be doing as well. I was intrigued by this girl's astute observation that talent did not always generate money, and sometimes less proficient people made a great deal of money. Of course, I was thinking that beyond having enough to sustain us, good food, shelter, a means to explore the world, developing friendships, and love, what else was so important?

While some may see that others have more material accouterments, some have less! I have discovered that attitude is indeed everything and often read what follows to my Reiki students.

ATTITUDE
By Charles Swindoll

The longer I live, the more I realize the impact of attitude on life.
Attitude, to me, is more important than facts.
It is more important than the past, than education, than
money, than circumstances, than failures, than successes,
than what other people think or say or do.

He goes on to say:

"The only thing we can do is play on the one
string we have, and that is our attitude.
I am convinced that life is ten percent what happens
to me and ninety percent how I react to it.
And so it is with you...we are in charge of our Attitudes."

After reflecting on this poem, I returned to my conversation with both women and introduced myself. Gloria told me she had four daughters. I am reminded, at the time of writing this story now years later, my daughter now has four daughters, including a pair of twin girls. Gloria expressed to me her interest in Kabbalah, which is an ancient wisdom that reveals how the Universe and life work. This philosophy assists in promoting better interactions between souls. Gloria then said she was aware that the Jewish mystics believed in codes in the Bible and that names and dates of births and deaths were part of that not-random code. All messages from Spirit give our lives greater direction and purpose according to a divine plan.

Gloria's daughter told me that before finding out her grandfather had passed on May 11 of the previous year, which also happened to be my mom's birth date, she had a dream of him. She woke up feeling anxious. Something was not right, but she thought this was the healthy grandfather and not the other grandfather who had health issues. She brushed aside her fears, only to find out in a few days that her fears were justified. Her healthy grandfather had died. Many of us receive information from Spirit in dream form, as Gloria's daughter did. This is a kind and practical way we may better deal with the difficult changes that occur unexpectedly in our lives and at the same time, discover a loving way that Spirit supports us while also reawakening us to remember our true state and nature as soul beings.

One story led to another, and Gloria had her own version of what she always thought to be a major coincidence but was finally realizing was never a coincidence. It was in regard to George Washington. I mentioned to Gloria the recent stories relating to George Washington that had presented themselves to me one after another in the last few weeks. I thought it to be curious that Gloria was also having some connections to George Washington. Gloria went on to describe her George Washington story. Weeks earlier, Gloria's friend, who was born on Washington's birth date, February 22nd, attended a brunch at the George Washington Manor. It was purported that Washington had stayed there during the Revolutionary War. Soon afterwards, Gloria was invited to dinner at the same George Washington Manor. I quickly remembered I also had dinner there on my birthday last year.

When I got to my office, later that same day, I picked up the local newspaper. There was an article with pictures of George Washington and his wife, Martha. The title was, "Washington Probably Infertile." The article said that historians felt that Washington's childlessness was a key to the country's stability at that time. After being part of the British monarchy, Americans did not want a similar form of succession to happen in America. It appears that the concept of monarchy and a ruling class in America that concerned our Founding Fathers still affects us now in 2016, when a president's son has already become a president and now an ex-president's wife runs for the office to perpetuate that concept of a ruling dynasty. It seems our Founding Fathers had not wanted that transfer and control of power to exist.

The timeliness of this article, in light of all the references to George Washington I was experiencing in the past several weeks, could be no coincidence. A connection between generations and past centuries was still very much a part of the ever-evolving story of our soul life and wondrous democratic government. The hopes of the Founding Fathers for our continued spiritual and political growth, which is so challenged now 250 years later, must still be appreciated.

It is now some time since I have reflected on these stories of George Washington, but recently I have been delighted to watch a clever and entertaining television series called "Sleepy Hollow," which is the story of Ichabod Crane, a British soldier who came to America and defected, becoming part of the American Army and a valuable advisor to George Washington. The show has many mystical references alluding to the fact that George Washington and some of the Founding Fathers had a higher evolved nature and were empowered by Spirit, and their main task was to set up a democratic system to lead the way for other nations of Earth to follow. The show alludes to the fact that we are at this very moment in what some would call the Apocalypse or the end of time: a fight between the good and evil energies of the Universe. Viewers are hopeful at the conclusion of every episode that Ichabod Crane and his entourage of police, scientists, spiritualists, and decent people will stem the tide of negativity and the destructive combative anger of so many disillusioned souls endangering our human way of life. And so hopefully we shall.

You may be wondering why I began this chapter with a line from The Declaration of Independence. Most historians, politicians, and educators might believe The Declaration of Independence is not a spiritual document. Much like The Ten Commandments and most biblical references, the needs of the soul require us to remember that freedom, or free will, is a divine gift and no one has the right to control our thoughts or actions. Freedom from fear and releasing limitations from each person's mental, physical, and spiritual features is the goal of the soul that has their own unique life plan, challenges, karma, and series of experiences that they will encounter along the way. Learning to throw off the shackles of fear and outdated beliefs so that inner values and a stronger connection to

Source may be followed always dwells within our hearts and is important in beginning anew.

> *Freedom is a right of public life and of our soul being, afforded*
> *by our Constitution, our Founding Fathers, and God.*

❖

It was another new day for me to visit hospice. I go each Tuesday like clockwork and have for eight years. Though I was asked only the other day by a colleague why I would want to volunteer for hospice, as he thought it was depressing, I responded simply, "Because I can." I also had seen the dedication and compassion hospice workers had shown my mother at the end of her life. Because I was not afraid of death or dying any longer, it seemed appropriate to use this newfound gift at hospice, where so much sorrow and fear still reside. It was also a great training ground for me to develop a greater sensitivity to the spiritual energies of various dimensions.

Eventually, I was more easily able to download messages from Spirit, from loved ones, spiritual guides, angels, or the souls of relatives for my clients. I came to see my ability as a way to help others access that unique, intuitive, divine part within them. It seemed I was a Soul Healer. In a hospice setting, Reiki energy and the kind intentions of a practitioner can help souls find closure, forgiveness, and validation for what has been good in their life. Spirit is also at work with them, helping to clear thoughts or fears before they journey to the Afterlife. All the hospice workers I have interacted with have had a similar mindset: to ease the patient gracefully and safely beyond these shores of physical life to their home beyond.

On this particular day, I was given a computer printout of seven names by one of the nurses. I visited the first man on the list, but he was sleeping. I sat only a few minutes at his side. Then, I decided to see the seventh person on the list. While it doesn't make sense that I skipped over the other names, when I entered the room, I understood why I was supposed to be there. The patient was a young woman who was extremely emaciated from her illness. Her mother was about to leave and was glad that I would stay with her daughter for a while.

The young woman, approximately 47 years old, was eating chocolate cake and had a wide smile on her face. I thought how difficult it was for her to be smiling and eating that cake, as she was so thin and fragile. I was immediately aware that she had little time left. She soon informed me that she had suffered from cancer, which was first discovered when she was pregnant 17 years ago, and since then had many treatments and surgeries. The struggle was long and hard, but she had lived long enough to see her first daughter in college and her son graduating from high school. She told me that from the time she was diagnosed with the illness, she had made her unrelenting intention and prayer to live long enough to raise her children.

Her daughter was now in a college that specialized in equestrian studies. This young woman I observed in her hospital bed had determination and strength of soul enforced by Spirit, which allowed her to relinquish a bit of her fears. She reminded me of the children we spoke of earlier who often lose their sense of innocence, develop fears through physical life challenges, and then, with the help of what may be angelic forces surrounding them or Spirit, remember once again either as a child or adult, that they are eternal souls who will reach beyond this short life experience to find love in a world that receives everyone.

Soon her husband walked in and introduced himself. "I'm Tim."

"You're Timothy?" I asked with amazement.

"Yes. I am Timothy, and my son is also Timothy." I mentioned to Tim that the many Timothy's I had met since the time of my mother's last illness and her passing had always shown to me that they were messengers from above. I related a few of the Timothy stories that had accumulated over the last few years and were always so comforting to me, offering me proof of a higher hand at work in our lives. I wanted to help Timothy recognize that people, much like angels or messengers from above, act as guides in the most difficult times of our lives. I told him that I believed the many men I had met with the name Timothy offered me solace and bolstered my faith and trust in a divine connection to Spirit.

The woman's husband Tim then said, "You have miraculous stories, and I have a story of a miracle also. My son, Timothy, who is now 18, was born after a five-and-a-half month pregnancy. He only weighed one pound.

He was a miracle baby and survived against all odds. Not only that, but he was written up in medical journals." Timothy told me his son is indeed a sweet, spiritual, loving person. In my mind, I felt that perhaps this baby was helped to live so that now he could help his mother die.

Then the young woman wanted to go to the bathroom and asked me if we could help her. I told her that we needed to ask the nurse, but she said they wouldn't allow it. Her husband and I helped her. Tim couldn't believe she did it. It wasn't this young woman's body that got her out of the bed. It was pure Spirit and soul. She was an amazing person. Before I left, she told me her father was waiting for her and she was going to be so happy to see him again. Earlier I had asked her if her father was in spirit, as I sensed someone waiting at the foot of her bed, smiling.

Driving home, I felt for a minute that I wanted to cry for her suffering. Then I realized crying would be for *my* sadness, and I should be cheering and applauding *her* triumph so I didn't cry too much and have written this story as a tribute to this young woman and her lovely husband, Timothy. Timothy stood by her side in a battle with disease and destiny.

Love stories that are truly great sometimes
seem to have a bittersweet ending.

In dealing with people's fragile thoughts of illness and death and in trying to alleviate pain or suffering in life, I have discovered it becomes helpful when we begin to utilize the tools of universal energy, or aware-ness, and a new perspective on what constitutes success.

Cindy Locher, one of the co-authors in *Mastering the Art of Success*, suggested, "Success for one woman might be a good marriage, happy children, and a career or area of study that she enjoys. Success for the man next door might mean a challenging job that keeps him on the run and provides enough money to enjoy life's amenities. Some people do not define success in terms of material gain. For those people, success means learning new things, growing spiritually and intellectually, and other altruistic ideals that are internal rather than external."

In today's competitive business world, success has become an art and those who master it are considered "lucky," but luck might not have as much to do with becoming successful as good, old-fashioned hard work and overcoming negative attitudes or people who limit you and your being able to learn, grow, or mature socially, spiritually, and emotionally.

Cindy also wrote, "Success is achieving your true potential despite our culture's portrayal of success as a life full of possessions and stature. People are learning that this may be a trap and that more things do not create a life that is emotionally and spiritually satisfying...it's been called the American Paradox—the more we have the more we want. Let's be very clear: for some people this will be the way they accept life and live their life, but for many they will find that their heart perhaps hurts or feels empty, and there is more to making them happy than what others have led them to believe. Money and possessions can't satisfy; they can only feed the need and that feeling of emptiness or question you often ask yourself...Isn't there more to life than this?"

It's the memoires, experiences, and love that fill a home, not the house itself. It is belonging and sharing mutual cooperation, finding your spiritual sense, discovering who you are and who you can be that will be the criteria for Success.

Gregg was in from California to celebrate St. Patrick's Day, a holiday he had always greatly loved. He was meeting all his boyhood friends at the St. Patrick's Day Parade in New York City, which, this year, was on the 22nd of March. At about one o'clock in the morning, I received a familiar call from Gregg, just like when he was a teenager. He said, "Mom, I'm on Maple Avenue. Could you come and get me?" His partying and the late hour had left him slightly overtired, so I jumped in the car, dressed in my robe and slippers, just like I had done years before. Some things never change, like love for your special son. When he got home, he told me he was the luckiest man in the world to wake up next to the most beautiful girl, Lea, whom he eventually married. Years after being diagnosed with diabetes, he had found love. He was, I believe, so grateful and protective of this new love. Perhaps having focused on the positive parts of his life, rather than the disease, he had become truly whole and well in his appreciation of his good fortune, and that is indeed a success for the soul mind and physical life he is living.

CHAPTER 4
Right Time, Right Place

*A little consideration of what takes place around us each day
would show us that a higher law than that of our will regulates
events…There is a soul at the center of nature and over the will
of every man so that none of us can wrong the universe.*
Ralph Waldo Emerson

I was on my way to visit one of the patients at hospice. Walking through the hallway, I met an attractive, tall couple in their sixties, and they were visiting their 92-year-old mother. As we talked, it became apparent to me that this was their second marriage or a new relationship. Marty told me how fortunate he had been to meet the new love of his life. Both their spouses had passed. They had been friends over the years and were lucky to find they cared deeply for each other. I suggested no relationship was random and it was part of their plan to be together at this time in their lives. All relationships, no matter how short or how long, have extreme value in our soul development. Soul growth, in my opinion, is a prime reason for a physical life, and relationships are the means for soul growth.

Marty then mentioned that he had a near-death experience after his heart had stopped during heart surgery. Marty found himself in a bright, sunlit meadow and felt no pain but felt physically great. He knew he had died, but after what seemed like a very short time, a voice told him he had to go back. Suddenly and abruptly, Marty was in the hospital, hearing all the equipment humming and hearing the doctors and nurses talking while operating on him. I told Marty my mother had a similar experience while in the hospital, and during her out-of-body experience, she had been told by a Spirit guide she had something to complete, and though she felt ready to remain in the quiet, lovely peaceful place she found herself in, she knew it was not yet her time.

Then Marty asked me if I believed in angels. In the earlier part of my life, I had not on a conscious level thought of angels as real and assumed angels to be a religious fabrication or a fairy-tale embellishment on our most fanciful and childish wishes. Not being particularly religious, I thought it a Christian concept and I was Jewish, so I didn't have enough knowledge on this subject. Here now, years later, after studying religion, philosophy, holistic healing, and ancient and modern takes on such subjects as angels, I am well aware that we all, through our personal relationship or experiences with the Divine, can find communication with angels. Angels can provide a clearer connection to Spirit, and *angels really do exist*. In my search, I became aware that a mystical group of the Jewish faith known as the Essences over 4000 years ago communicated with angels and believed in an afterlife, so it was not a new belief 2000 years later, when Jesus delivered his message of eternal love and life as a messenger of God. Mary, Jesus's mother, was most possibly a student of this mystical Essences group and was chosen as a young child and advised, in time, of her future as the mother of a messenger of eternal life—her son, Jesus—by an angel who actually delivered God's message to her.

Throughout religious documentation, prophets and
messengers have been advised by angels, who bring the
wisdom and guidance of God to the physical realm.

As a result of feeling the power and love of angelic strength and determination as their energy sometimes dances around me, I know their divine presence is a powerful force for healing in the Universe. Furthermore, I also believe angels may present as actual physical people to help others in compromising situations. After expressing that idea to Marty, he told me another amazing story of how his car had broken down near an airport one night. A man he could not accurately describe took him all the way home to Levittown. Marty hadn't been feeling well, and the road was pitch-black and deserted. This man just appeared in his car and automatically helped him. I believe almost everyone could dig into the deep recesses of their memories and extract a similar moment of unexpected and blessed help.

When Marty and his wife went into her mother's room, they asked me to join them. They told me how stupendous she was. Indeed, though she was 92 years old and fragile, she had a bright smile on her face. I took her hand and introduced myself. "Hi, I'm Sheryl, and 'I'm so happy to meet you. Your children tell me you are an incredible woman." She responded as she held my hand, "I love you," and then kissed my hand. I could tell she had lived a life in that loving way and was at peace.

She couldn't quite hear anything being said, but she was alert and aware of where she was and not afraid of where she was going. "What is your name?" I asked.

"Frances."

"Well, Frances, I just met two women with the name Francine, and that's close to your name. Three friends in a row is a sign of good fortune. I wish you peace and love, and should you meet my mom, her name is Ceil. Please say hello for me." I said goodbye to the family, and her daughter told me that the good I was bringing to so many made me a special person.

It might be possible that I am a special person these days, as I love myself for being able to give to most people a little piece of the love that God has inspired within me. I am no longer afraid of other people's opinions or their judgments, and I am most grateful to greet each new day, adventure, and activity with courage and hope. If a tear or two wells up in my eye, as it often does, I'm equally grateful for being able to feel in a world that often tries to stifle caring and generosity. Winning for me now means acceptance of my destiny and acceptance of the many people around me I love, even though their road may take them in a different direction than mine.

❖

About a month ago, a medium told me that I would be attending a bat mitzvah. I couldn't think of anyone who would be inviting me to one in the near future. Several weeks later, my niece Robin called and asked me to come to her temple's 40th-anniversary party. She especially wanted my husband and me there. "Of course," I said. A few days before the event, she called me and told me that it was indeed the temple's 40th-anniversary party, but she really wanted me to attend her bat mitzvah. She had not wanted her parents to know, as it was a surprise. Robin, unbeknownst to me, had been studying for the last year and a half.

The night of the bat mitzvah arrived. The three women, who were also having their bat mitzvah that night, were incredibly well-prepared, articulate, and accomplished women who took time out of their busy lives to seek an ancient connection to God. Listening to my niece Robin was a moving experience for me, and I felt my mother, father, and family-in-Spirit were present. I sensed my mom crying for Robin's success and perseverance. I also cried as my mother cried in the upper world.

I had until this time been the only light in our family pursuing spiritual awareness and an awakening process. Now there were two of us. Perhaps all my talk about life surviving physical death and an afterlife had motivated Robin to pursue her own connection to divine energy and to her grandmother, whom she loved dearly and missed. When I told Robin that I felt her grandmother was present and so proud of her, she said she hoped so. Then she said to me, "You are the one person in the family I most needed to be here."

What we do to improve ourselves with an open mind,
effort, and love, improves all who are joined to us.

After the service, we proceeded to Robin's house, where she had a tent set up in the backyard. Caterers were floating all around, preparing and serving food. It was chilly for a June summer night, but I was thoroughly enjoying the festivities. There were children, a mangy dog, and lots of grown-ups and noise. It wasn't long before my husband asked me to come over to meet a couple he was talking to. The woman's name was Debbie, and her husband was Jeff. Debbie had a round face and a sweet personality. She told me she had grown up in my hometown, Rockville Centre, and her mom and dad were Mimi and Mel. I laughed, because they were tag-sales specialists whom I had known when we were all in the same business long ago. Even though we were competitors, we were all teachers and were friendly, and there was enough work for all of us. Like me, Debbie's mom and dad were involved in new pursuits but really had loved the work and people they met and helped while in that experience of transition for the homeowners moving to new places and challenges.

The next day, after the festivities of Robin's party, I needed to feel the warmth of the sun at the ocean, and I proceeded to Long Beach. I sat on a bench on the boardwalk facing the pounding, breaking waves. The sun danced in and out of the clouds, and there weren't too many people on the beach in this particular spot. I noticed the dedication on the bench where I sat down. It was dated "September 11, 2001, American flight 77. George W. and Diane M. always in our thoughts, forever in our hearts. We will always remember life is good."

I am reminded by the words embossed on the brass plaque on this bench of the recent references to George Washington, our first president. Spirit in my heart tells me that George Washington was an evolved spiritual leader who heralded in a new age of fair thinking and equalitarianism. I look now to the controversial 2016 political arena and hope to see a person with fair-minded qualities again grace our political stage and rekindle the dignity of earlier days when communication, family, and fair trade were attributes to forge lives lived in harmony, balance, and for the most part, peace. Of course, now with the earth supporting over eight billion people, our resources are more limited. We must begin to conserve and work cooperatively to supply water and food and share what we can to protect as many people as we can. However, I also know there is enough for all of us, and we must choose to focus on that positive state of being as we hold the thoughts of prosperity and well-being.

At the same time, for some reason, I remembered the final words of my mother before she passed. "I ate a good breakfast, I love you, and life has been good." The beauty of these simple but true thoughts touches me. I am happy that my mother learned three of the most important reasons for a physical life, which are joy, happiness, and sustaining yourself with what you need to survive, but not overdoing it.

I moved to the bench next to the one I was sitting on. I always love to read the inscriptions. This one was dedicated to survivors of 9/11. It read: "The best bunch of guys you would ever want to meet. Real friends are the ones who walk in when the rest walk out. Friends are forever." Then there were three plaques listing all the firemen who had survived the ordeal and devastation of the Twin Towers.

About six months ago, David saw a film that he was most taken with. It was called *The Walk*, a biographical drama depicting a high-wire artist from France, Philippe Petit, who lived life by defying death and following his aspiration as he pursued his seemingly impossible dream to walk on a tightrope attached to the north and south towers of the World Trade Center. With the help from his amazing and encouraging friends and his trainer, Petit attempted the impossible, guided by his soul and his Spirit. On August 7, 1974, Petit walked between the two imposing high towers, completing a task that seemed death-defying to all. David told me to see this movie at least four times when it was in the theatre, but for various reasons, I was unable to do so. Many months later while doing a reading for Claire, a member of my meditation group, I felt a spirit beside me crying, and I began to cry also as I saw the Twin Towers in glistening light in all of their original splendor and intuitively knew that the souls that left that day all still lived beyond this earth plane. Claire told me I was connecting to her high-school friend who passed away during the collapse of Twin Towers. After that reading, I went home and turned on the television and discovered *The Walk* was playing. I watched the entire movie and was surprised that David had loved it so much, as it was more an art film and spiritual story rather than merely a survival story, a genre he is fond of. *The Walk* was poetic, artistic, not your average, everyday film. For me, it clearly portrayed a soul's journey and a truly loving group of people with all the most noble values and motivations. After his triumphant walk, Philippe Petit was given a lifetime pass to climb to the top of any New York building to see the Twin Towers in the distance, and for years he did that. At the end of the movie, I couldn't believe what I saw. After 9/11, Philippe was looking in the direction of the Twin Towers, sadly remembering all the people who were gone, and saw the Towers still standing just like I saw in Claire's reading. It was the exact image! I believe we both saw the Towers in Spirit, beautifully full of light and life, offering us the promise that all that we love in life that is good is never gone but transcends to a higher place.

Wherever there may be loss and sadness, there will also be many blessings, which offer us hope and sustain us in the wisdom that we are truly alive, whether in the physical world or beyond.

❖

I had a session with a woman who had lost her husband on 9/11. Sometimes if a client asks me a question while undergoing a Reiki session, I am able, through a visual symbol, feeling, or thought, to sense an answer. This client asked if her husband had suffered during his death. I immediately experienced extreme heat from the fire of the jet fuel that had rammed into one of the towers. I also sensed how quickly his soul had left his body. Tears were streaming down my face as I internalized the sadness and extreme sorrow, he experienced at leaving his wife and children while knowing they would miss him. His anguish ran through me. Somehow, I mentioned that at the Boardwalk the day before, I thought someone had crept up behind me, and I was scared in that moment, but when I looked around, there was nobody there. My client exuberantly said her husband often did that to friends and family. Intuitively, I knew that he was aware his wife would see me the next day, so he cleverly presented himself to me the day before, hoping I would tell her the story. It was his way of validating he was always or forever near to his wife.

CHAPTER 5
Our Divine Struggles

Great minds have purpose; others have wishes.
Washington Irving

Today is June 27th, and it is my older sister Rodelle's birthday. I like to think my mom-in-spirit directed me to sit on these two benches on the boardwalk in Long Beach in order to pick up an understanding of our family's issues and the needs of other people I interact with. Whatever the reason, I am always grateful for the help Spirit offers me. At times I often feel like a child who cannot climb even a small step alone but still tries independently, as we are often guided to do by our parents, even when help is close by. Now I am learning we can always raise our eyes to the heavens and ask for whatever help we need. My sister Rodelle became ill with pancreatic cancer and chose to have chemotherapy. In watching my sister battle with this insidious disease, it was necessary for me to draw on the guidance and love from my spiritual loved ones to calm the sadness surrounding the suffering I had to watch Rodelle endure. Over the year and a half of treatments, her will to live and her spirit to trust never wavered. As a volunteer for hospice, I observed many people pass from pancreatic cancer, so I knew the pain was excruciating. So, each night, I sent Reiki energy and prayers to Rodelle, asking that she have the least amount of pain possible. Over the course of her many treatments, I always asked her if she had much pain, and she always responded, "No." Rodelle's love of life was supported by her many friends and family, her work, her enthusiasm for fashion, and her interest in exploring this beautiful world by travelling to many exotic, tropical locations and historical places. These interests and passions worked to sustain her through the many setbacks and complications of the treatment plan she had opted for. As a holistic practitioner, I had wanted her to try alternative treatments such as Chinese herbal medicine, acupuncture, hyperthermia that kills cancer cells but does not weaken the immune system, and other energy-healing methods. Of course, I am aware that approximately 98 percent of people with a diagnosis of metastasized cancer do not survive with chemotherapy or perhaps with any other treatments. I know there was little that the system or the protocols of The American Medical Association could do other than follow their formula for treatment, but I believe after 40 years of chemotherapy producing ultimately the same results and loss of life for a good number of patients, patients should be offered all options available, not only those approved by the FDA. Improvements and advanced knowledge by the doctors should be offered, and patients should be told of all complications surrounding different treatments so they can eventually make a personal decision for how to face their challenge and ultimate ending. A person who is diagnosed with cancer is initially filled with fear and dread and will usually follow the first plan of treatment offered. It seems prudent to me to receive at least two to three opinions before embarking on any treatment plan, and we should incorporate a host of modalities and treatments to assist anyone dealing with a serious or terminal illness.

Laurie Beck, author of *Living to Tell*, a cancer survivor, and a guest on *Healing from Within*, supports the idea that it is necessary to get more than one opinion before embarking on a treatment plan. Laurie was diagnosed with two forms of cancer: non-Hodgkin's B lymphoma and leukemia. The first doctor she consulted wished to begin an immediate regime of what is known as "the chop," a very intensive form of chemotherapy. The second doctor consulted suggested she immediately begin chemotherapy. However, Laurie's mother, who was a motivational speaker on the subject of stress and believed that stress, lifestyle, and emotional patterns from childhood often created illness and dysfunction in the body, insisted that her daughter go to the Dana-Farber Cancer Institute in Boston, Massachusetts. Laurie went and met Dr. David Fisher, who shook Laurie's hand and very causally asked, "So, how do you feel?" Laurie responded, "Well, I used to feel good until I was told I had some rare, chronic, no-cure disease that seems to be getting worse each time I go to a different doctor." After seeing three doctors, it was confirmed Laurie did have two types of cancer. Laurie asked Dr. Fisher, "What would you do if you were in my shoes?" Dr. Fisher responded, "Well, we need to save your magic bullets. The magic bullet is chemo, and it is anything but magic. 'Stopgap' is more like it. Chemo might get rid of it for a while, but there is a good chance it will return." Laurie writes in *Living to Tell*, "Chemo basically destroys all the good cells in the body while trying to terminate the bad cells. It weakens your immune system, leaving you extremely vulnerable. The chemo cocktail protocol was considered the strongest and potent available... Ah, no wonder Dr. Fisher called them the magic bullets. You load the gun, take a shot, and it's hit or miss." Dr. Fisher asked three very important questions: "Do you have night sweats, have you lost a lot of weight lately, and do you feel extremely tired?" When Laurie responded "No, not really," Dr. Fisher told Laurie she could go home and do what is called "watchful waiting." "In other words, we aren't going to do anything for the moment. We're going to just wait to see what happens." Dr. Fisher asked Laurie to come back in three months to have blood work and a CT scan. In the interim, Laurie embarked on a holistic program including Reiki, acupuncture, Chinese medicine, herbal therapy, Tai Chi, meditation, prayer, and being in nature more. Laurie continued on a regime of helping her body and mind to relax and let go of former issues, stresses, and patterns that were not helpful to her wellbeing and recovery. She changed her thinking and attitudes, finding gratitude and greater love. When she returned to Dr. Fisher to have her blood test and CT scan, she heard Dr. Fisher say, "We'll see you in three months. No chemo again." She knew she had more time to simply be. Eventually, by Laurie following her natural, holistic regimen and without using chemotherapy, Dr. Fisher was able to report that both cancers were in remission and Laurie was healthy.

A recent article in *Time Magazine* about breast cancer also suggests doctors are working with a "wait and see" therapy before going to the final stage of long-term chemo with all its side effects. This October 2015 article in *Time Magazine*, entitled "Why Doctors are Rethinking Breast-Cancer Treatment," suggested too much chemo, too much radiation, and way too many mastectomies are being prescribed. Dr. Shelley Hwang, mentioned in the article, supports some breast-cancer patients who choose to do "active surveillance" rather than invasive procedures or chemotherapy that will weaken the immune system further, as it is known that the body has the ability to self-heal and eliminate toxic situations if given a chance. Active surveillance, like the "wait and see" approach used in Laurie Beck's treatment, is an approach involving routine tests and monitoring on a set schedule with your doctor, in lieu of more immediate aggressive treatment. Many less invasive types of cancer treatments might work, and a patient might never progress to a life-threatening situation.

Whatever choices for treatment that a person makes in terms of dealing with their illness must be respected, as their soul ultimately knows, on a subconscious level, their journey and life plan. In the future, many people hope there will be more integrative medical approaches bridging allopathic and alternatives treatments to deal with serious health issues. I have spent the last two years of my sister's terminal illness researching and interviewing people who had survived their cancer diagnosis using alternative methods. While unfortunately, this information was not able to help my sister, who was totally committed to the Western form of medicine—chemotherapy, radiation surgeries and medication—and not completely open to the many alternative methods that exist, as we move forward, we will hopefully learn that keeping a person alive at any cost and consequence may not be as humane as keeping them comfortable, using less invasive treatments, and allowing for a fair-to-good quality of life for as long as possible.

As always, we should have choices, but our choices can only be based on the knowledge we are given and also on our life plan, karma, and soul needs.

Rodelle made her choices based on her reality and totally accepting her doctor's choices but regardless of her failing health, pretty much maintained her normal routine, even traveling to her favorite place, Aruba, a month before she passed. Her doctors kept telling her she did not look sick, and right after her last birthday celebration, when her body could no longer sustain the chemotherapy treatments, she was admitted to a clinical trial that she had been anxious to participate in. It was too late for that to work in her favor. On my last visit with her at her home, I asked her to tell me the message she would send if indeed either she or I found ourselves beyond life to be still alive...even though she was not as sure as I was that there was a life waiting for her. We decided that every time I saw a fluffy, sweet-faced, white Bichon dog like her dog, Oliver, she would be saying hello to me. Soon after her passing, I was watching television, and a small white dog like Oliver, with his leg wrapped in a blue bandage, unable to move quickly, stopped to see the other dogs move so freely and fast. Sadly, the small dog walked up to his owner, a dark haired, sensitive-looking, otherworldly young man, and looked into his eyes, and immediately the man seemed inspired. He opened his cell phone to order a carrier so his dog could be carried close to his heart and loved till he healed. The words sung at the end of the commercial were, "I was born among the stars." That was, I think, a great message from my very clever sister letting me know she and all our loved one's dance in eternal life.

Imagination, intuition, and trust allow many of us to think outside of the box and find divinity and magic in the arts. There is always more that the eye can see or know. My desire to observe love in all its mysteriousness and nuances led me to the Spider-Man movie series. I was delighted to attend the opening of Spider-Man 2. I had been waiting to see it since the first edition, when I noticed so much synchronicity to my own life. The messages of responsibility, love, dedication, change, and loss are common themes we all deal with. We are also able to see that many people have a limited view of the nature of the soul. Spider-Man is a soulful, spiritual movie allowing us to discover the beauty and intensity of soul life as we learn that the soul's needs are the navigating force creating our life and all of our challenges. Since the human soul is the light that creates our daily experiences, it is sometimes blocked by egotistical thoughts of our mind. You see, the ego is not actually your true self. It is your soul that is the true and everlasting, ever-growing essence and holder of all memories and all lives. Often the soul must struggle to bring its light and wisdom into sync with the thoughts and desires of the ego or physical world.

I feel that the Spider-Man movies are a must-see for those follow-ing an inner path of self-discovery, intent on trying to send and receive unconditional love from the soul, rather than realizing love from merely an ego-based viewpoint. This movie, along with other experiences, has helped me realize life is too often viewed from either the egotistical state of mind or world consciousness, as opposed to from the soul or inner state of connection to Higher Self. Thinking about this has led me to know it is not in the separation of our physical and spiritual life but in the non-duality, or oneness of our being, the merging of our ego and soul, that we come to really understand who we are, where we come from, and where we will return.

All great art, literature, theater, and music, indeed any
creative expression, seeks to bring these divine, inspirational
revelations of beauty and connectedness into reality.

Life continued to be good for so many of us. I was reminded of that today after a difficult hospice visit with a young woman who was only 44 years old and dying from cancer. Of course, she was frightened and worried about leaving her young daughter. I held her hand and told her she was not alone, as there were so many loving and helpful people around her. She experienced some pain and became quite agitated, so I called for a nurse, who responded immediately and administered medication. The patient wanted me to stay in her room and told me that my presence had a calming effect on her. It was a long afternoon. I was saddened by the young woman's condition, though I maintained a cheerful and light manner for her benefit. I knew it must be in her best interest in the whole scope of her soul's journey for her to be experiencing this untimely illness. We cannot know all the reasons for illness, loss, and sadness and how they figure into the larger scheme of the divine energy plan we each have, but I firmly believe that this patient would find joy and health beyond her terminal illness and would be finally in a place where her soul would be with loved ones to continue her soul's journey.

We will come to know we are an eternal force of
continuous life, and there is no ending to soul being.

❖

Some people think mediums are going against the doctrines of certain religions, and this way of thinking concerns me greatly, as they are rejecting the gifts that God gives all of us through an awareness of a God Consciousness and a love for life and truth, as He raises our consciousness to find our soul divinity. Throughout the earliest recordings of miracles, devoted people have worked to follow God's messages, to be closer to the Spiritual realms, to help people deal with the human condition, and to create a prosperous, healthy lifestyle worthy of Spirit's hopes for humanity. I believe mediums receive their gift from this divine, intelligent energy source and are born to serve. As people mature, look past right and wrong concepts, and accept themselves and the world, they come to know peace and through prayer, meditation, and study, forge a more intimate relationship with the divine so their connection to God deepens.

We will be approaching the next election in 2020 before too long, and though the loss of confidence in our government, congress, and corporate life leaders surrounding the unhinged, judgmental behaviors seen as a result of the outcome of the 2016 election not accepted by some have persisted, it has become clear to me that our guides and angels are standing at our side to open our awareness to higher consciousness and help us find ways of relating in more loving and responsible ways by moving past hatred and anger. I recently was asked to be a guest at the Enlightened Women Enlightened You Summit hosted by Dr. Ruth Anderson, who told me that Archangel Michael was part of 500,000 light beings on the planet at the present time to aid us in our movement through all the tragedies and heartaches we are experiencing now to a more loving, peaceful time for humanity. I immediately tried to connect to the energy of these teachers and angels being so moved by their desire to help with the healing of our many problems. It is through miracles that they will work with humanity at this troubling time for many people to open their hearts. The reading that follows is what was expressed to me.

April 30, 2019

A march across the valley through mountains

Side by side, row after row, endless power and discipline to walk the world as the Jewish people walked through the Red Sea and desert to find God

We will help you triumph in light and be free

We begin with the children and lift them up to hold their own sense of goodness and help the elders be more aligned to their own innocence

We will fan and cool the rage and anger with "Miracles"

Like the boy who lives after being thrown off from the highest point of an escalator in a mall in Minnesota

And the Rabbi who with love blesses the woman who gave her life to save him during a shooting in the temple so he could speak the truth to his congregation and nation thanking the President of the United States who gave his time effort and blessings to help the Jewish people and to end hatred and return us to peace.

The women and angels like lifting a tree from a sprout to a giant timber will encourage nurturing Women's Rights and their nature to provide the best of their life force so the planet can stand married to life love and new beginnings

The pain of relationship will be given up for more interactive processes and we will insist on equality for Men and Women, Black Brown and White, Jewish Christian or Islam

We will insist on allowing groups to meet and find common ground

It is not a request, but a Divine Decree!

❖

Yesterday, August 14, 2019, in Philadelphia during a police intervention of a drug-related event, a lone gunman, a criminal, kept the entire police force at bay for an entire day before surrendering. The media called it a "miracle" that six policemen were wounded but lived and the gunman was arrested without being killed. We must continue to be aware of the changes that are happening in everyday life and see that goodness has a strong possibility of beating the odds no matter how daunting.

Religious leaders can offer their own interpretations and personal feelings. One such marvelous religious leader, Reverend Michael J.S. Carter, whom I recently interviewed, expressed in simple words his love for Spirit and the reason that we are on this planet. He wrote, "I believe that the reason we are on this planet is to serve humanity and to learn to love and to forgive ourselves as well as others. The Spirit of All Life that resides in us resides in every living thing, and this Spirit is what connects us to all of life. Put another way, the cultivation of our inner lives is what keeps us connected and does away with the illusion that we are separated from each other and the natural world."

> *Knowing "all is as it is" for each soul as they discover*
> *resilience, a capacity to love, and a higher connection*
> *to their own spirit is the key to acceptance.*
> *It is when you are really living in the present—working,*
> *thinking, lost, absorbed in something you care about*
> *very much—that you are living spiritually.*
>
> Brenda Ueland

CHAPTER 6
Welcome, My Granddaughter

Every man's life is a fairy-tale written with God's fingers.
Hans Christian Andersen

The baby was almost here. On Friday, April 15, 2005, Stacey and Jeremy's baby girl was due to arrive, and I was on standby waiting for the phone call. Upon receiving a call from Jeremy, I immediately drove to Mount Sinai in New York City. Stacey had been in labor since four o'clock in the morning. Jeremy said the baby would be here soon and everything was going well.

My son Gregg, was coming in from California that night. The baby was waiting for him to arrive. Funny, I think, but the night my mom passed, Gregg had just arrived at the airport from London. She also waited for him to come home before her passing.

My medium friends told me that I intimately knew this old soul who would soon be my first granddaughter. I was anxious to welcome her into the world and to assist my daughter in having a comfortable delivery, so I continued to send distant healing Reiki energy while driving.

When I arrived at the hospital, they immediately sent me to the second floor. I asked the nurse if I could see my daughter, Stacey Glick. She said in a solemn voice, "Are you the mother? Right this way!" I got scared and asked, "Is she all right? The nurse didn't respond.

I followed her, walking briskly into the room, and saw Stacey holding this tiny wrapped bundle. Stacey said, "I can't believe she's ours." I looked at the baby and immediately saw the resemblance to Jeremy, her father. She was beautiful. They named her Samantha Emma. I just kept looking at the baby, and while she was small at 6 pounds, 4 ounces and 20 inches long, she did make it to her exact due date. Several medium friends had told me she would be born prematurely, but perhaps all the prayers and energy healing from myself and my group encouraged the baby to wait full term so she could be healthy and safe. My daughter was upset that I told her the baby might be early, and while that prediction helped her get things done quickly, it also frightened us.

I decided as a result of this miscalculated message from another medium that in the future, I would not reveal any messages but those that were given to me personally by Spirit. Once again, Spirit was asking me to use my divine good judgment and trust myself.

> *It is my fond intention that each of us begins to respect*
> *and love our self and to rely on our own intuition to make*
> *choices that bring us great positivity and joy in life.*

As a result of the trauma my daughter experienced from that miscalculation I was given, I decided to make some firm rules for the way I disseminated information from Spirit, as future predictions, if interpreted incorrectly by the medium, might influence the choices one makes and might take away a client's free will. Ultimately our journey and the decisions we make must be our own, while psychic impressions are better used to help people clarify, validate, and refine their own thinking. Through messages from mediums, Spirit allows us to trust ourselves and make our own choices. We are not puppets being played by the Universe for their amusement but are allowed to develop greater awareness and evolve at our own pace. The success or failure of any action is often connected to original soul intentions that may have possibly been overlooked or forgotten for the moment. Mediums may discover over time that an exaggerated or enhanced message could unintentionally create self-fulfilling prophecies, and they should be most careful not to embellish or put their own spin on any message.

My mentors have thankfully impressed on me that there is a delicacy in relaying certain messages. No medium who is well trained should ever tell someone that they see death for that person, even if they do. Ultimately the time of passing is holy and only decided by a higher power.

> *The plan of life and death can be altered by metaphysical*
> *conditions. Ultimately, we simply listen to the small, quiet divine*
> *voice within ourselves and make choices to the best of our ability.*

❖

I knew through observation and intuition my beautiful granddaughter Samantha Emma would be strong-willed, independent, fearless, and filled with honor. Of course, like all of us, she would also be filled with moments of self-doubt about life and her life purpose. However, I did not know the old soul she had been when I looked into her eyes, even though I so wished to remember our connection from before. I just knew that she was a gift from God.

Days after Samantha's birth, I was at my nail salon in Hewlett, and the woman next to me was expecting her first grandchild in July. I heard her talking about it and told her I just had a granddaughter born on April 15th. She said both of her nieces had their sons on April 15 and they were three weeks early. Odd, I thought, that I was told that my granddaughter would be early, and here is a woman telling me about two babies who were *actually* born early.

I told this woman, Barbara, that she glowed with good health, and she said that was only because she had a strong spiritual sense. Actually, she told me she was a type 1 diabetic for 31 years and had been using the insulin pump these last five years. "Well," I said, "we have another coincidence." My son, Gregg is also using the pump for the most effective monitoring of his insulin needs. She told me her husband was a pediatric doctor and should have been in a wheelchair, but due to wonderful coincidences, he had escaped that prognosis. Barbara then asked for my business card. At that very moment I thought about my dad-in-spirit, whom I believed was supposed to be bringing people to me who shared stories of synchronicity, but it had been quiet for a little bit, so I assumed he was slacking off on his job. Dad was back on the job!

❖

The next day at work, I picked up the *East Rockaway Herald* and noticed an article entitled "A Verity Memoir." The picture showed a young priest who had served for 28 years and then left his ministry to marry a woman named Ceil. That was mom's name. The former priest had three daughters, as had my mom and dad. The synchronicity and the title of the book the former priest had written, *Meant to Be*, captured my attention.

The article mentioned that on March 15th of last year, James G. Verity completed writing his memoirs. The project had taken ten years. He and his wife were scheduled to celebrate their 35th wedding anniversary. James didn't quite feel up to snuff and checked into Saint Frances Hospital. The former priest passed away several weeks later, and his family used their own funds to publish his book. The messages of faith, love, and tolerance his book tried to show that *everything happens for a reason.*

In the foreword section of his book, James stated, "I don't believe that people walk in and out of our lives purposelessly. Nor do I believe that events planned or unplanned happen completely without rhyme or reason."

My own life experience and connection to God or divine energy have brought me to much the same conclusion.

CHAPTER 7
Bridge the Gap Between Both Worlds

When you arise in the morning, think of what a precious privilege
it is to be alive—to breathe, to think, to enjoy, to love.
Marcus Aurelius

My office was closed during this Memorial Day weekend. I had several errands to complete before driving to visit my daughter and her family in Brooklyn Heights. This very quaint, distinctive, renovated section of New York, with its fantastic turn-of-the-century brownstones and lots of fun activities like outdoor fairs, food fests, and holiday rides for the children and adults, was heavily populated, and there was lots of activity going on. I thought I would stop at the car wash, but I also wanted to stop at the baby-furniture store where my husband and I had purchased the crib and dressing table for Samantha. I had promised Stacey I would try to get a slipcover for the baby's rocking chair. All of a sudden, the car seemed to turn around, physically and abruptly, matching my sudden decision to forgo the car wash. I drove back a few blocks to the baby-furniture store.

The store must have just opened. There were no cars in front. I parked and entered the store, and a mature but youthful-looking woman with dark hair approached me.

"Hello, I'd like a slipcover for a rocking chair that I purchased in this store," I said.

"These covers are all custom-made and have to be ordered," she said.

"Do you have any in the store today that I might purchase? I would like to bring one to my daughter today."

She went in the back to look and came out with two choices. Both were very nice but also expensive. I told her how nice she was to try so hard to accommodate me and then asked her name.

" Harriet," she responded.

"That's funny," I said. "For years my husband has called me Harriet as a joke, and I used to get so annoyed at his sense of humor. As an energy healer and medium, I am aware of past lives and different experiences that lead us to either be comfortable or uncomfortable with certain situations... Perhaps in another time or place, I was Harriet."

"What a coincidence! My daughter just had a reading with someone on the North Shore. I think his name is Jeffrey Wands."

I had met Jeffrey recently. Little by little, as my abilities developed over the last ten years, I have met many of the mediums who are out there working. They are a small, select group, and I imagine that like-minded people do eventually cross paths.

Harriet related a very intimate story to me. She lost her son when he was 16 years old. He was at a rock concert at Nassau Coliseum and running across the road with his friend. He was hit by a car and instantly killed. His friend was not hurt. Her story immediately triggered a memory of when my daughter Stacey was 15 and had gone to Nassau Coliseum to hear a U2 concert. When she told me she wanted to go, I had a strong, uncomfortable gut feeling that this was not a good idea and thought that there could be drinking and wildness, and I had a feeling they would all be running and she would be trampled. Stacey was petite, and I was not comfortable with her going, but as always, she was fearless and alleviated my fears by telling me her two very tall and mature friends would be with her. Not wanting her to miss out on her fun, I squelched my own negative fears and sent her on her adventure.

Later that night when Stacey returned, I saw from my bedroom window that she was limping toward the front door. My stomach dropped, as I saw she was injured. She told me she was running in the parking lot and fell on a metal rod coming out of the road. Thank God all she needed was a tetanus shot. To this day she has a hole in that leg.

My attention returned to Harriet, who continued to say that a message from a medium shortly after her son's death had implied her son was trying to find a way back to her. Years later, her daughter adopted a baby girl and named her Samantha.

"That's my new granddaughter's name," I said. I knew by now that it was no coincidence that I was talking to Harriet.

"Well," continued Harriet, "right after Samantha was adopted, my daughter had triplets and was so busy with them that I took care of Samantha. We are so close. She has green eyes like my son, Stephen. Samantha has brought me so much joy and love."

"Many times," I said, "when I have clients come to me for the first time and I give them messages from loved ones who were on the other side, they just cry." They often can feel the energy and know their loved one is near. With that, Harriet started to cry, and I realized even though she believed Samantha had the soul of her son, the hurt from the loss so long ago was still painful for her.

Harriet went to another drawer and found a pale pink cover set for the rocking chair and said, "This was one of the originals that is no longer being made."

I purchased it and replied, "My daughter, Stacey will enjoy this."

"Your daughter's name is Stacey? My daughter's name is also Stacey!"

❖

Each time I visited Samantha, I learned so much from our time together... For me, being with children always takes me on a trip back to my own childhood and also to the time when I was raising my own children. What I may not have experienced, understood, or valued then is, in this time of my life, a new opportunity to learn, move past limiting thoughts, and find happiness. Today as I took care of Samantha, I noticed her eyes were incredibly trusting and thoughtful. Her cooing sounds seemed almost like words to me. When it was time for her nap, I put her in her crib and arranged some musical toys so she wouldn't feel alone. Then I went out of the room. She made playful sounds for about 15 minutes. Then I sensed she was getting ready to cry. She saw me and made a face like she would cry if I didn't pick her up. So, I picked her up, and there was no crying.

In my estimation, there is no need for an infant or young child to cry in fear if their needs are met before they are actually desperate enough to cry. Books may tell you that a fourth trimester baby is still a fetus and in many physical ways, their reflexes are only automatic. However, I maintain a belief that the baby's soul is quite astute in its spiritual awareness of the environment and the people caring for them. All babies are learning information about their caretakers and the world around them. Talking to them intelligently and constantly explaining what you are doing can help them be comfortable and feel safe. I believe this is the right approach for dealing with infants and young children. Developing well-adjusted babies who feel secure and trusting and have a positive approach to life is definitely influenced by the care and attention they receive early on. It is well documented that unattended babies become fearful and develop into children who are not comfortable in their own physical bodies. This creates difficulties both physically and emotionally that may challenge them their entire lifetime.

Caring for your child is more than attending to their physical safety or wellbeing... It is being attentive to and respecting their soul wisdom and soul needs.

Friendships ebb and flow. We continue to meet new people as we journey forward. Wherever we share a connection of friendship or love, it remains forever viable in the higher energy field of Spirit.

❖

We must walk in balance on the earth, a foot in Spirit and a foot in the physical.
Lynn Andrews, 20th Century American Writer and Shaman

Once we truly are able to feel and listen to both our spiritual companions in life and those beyond this earth plane, the meaning of who we are will become clearer. It has become clearer to me that we are indeed physical and also spiritual beings, four-dimensional, resonating and vibrating through our own thoughts, creating the totality of our life situations. Debra Diamond, a guest on *Healing From Within* and author of *Life After Near Death*, explores the idea of consciousness in relationship to her experiences. Debra is clairvoyant and downloads messages from Spirit and wrote, "Our consciousness absorbs everything during our lifetime. Yet, consciousness occupies a realm of no time and no space. There is no past, present, or future as far as consciousness is concerned. When we are in our earthly bodies, we cannot fathom this since our earthly bodies experience events sequentially and linearly through our physical senses. This creates our reality. Yet, when we are free of our physical body, we experience hyper-real perception and ultra-clarity. Our consciousness is able to register everything happening in the Universe with total clarity unencumbered by our physicality."

This state of consciousness may be experienced while asleep. When in dreams we transcend this physical body and are in contact with our eternal true being or Higher Self, we are connected to the cosmic forces of an ever-evolving creative Universe, as we are ever-evolving souls and part of that energetic force. Our soul energy is therefore free to lift up from our restrictive bodies and to relax, renew, and explore endless possibilities. This concept may be partially explained by some as an out-of-body experience.

Only a true blending of the better aspects of both realities helps us to restore our soul being in its entirety. At this time in human history, the world seems to be ablaze with the passions and furies of so many different cultures and religious or political mindsets, many primed to disregard or exploit the commonality of our humanness and fracture our ability to merge the best of human history and its outer-world reality. I have long hoped that as people rediscover their true inner essence, they will move past the definitions of themselves as merely physical beings who only survive in what often seems a terrifying and challenging world and will come to know that as all religions, cultures, ethnic groups, genders, and political activities come together, the pieces of a universal puzzle, including unity and oneness, will move us past separation and divisiveness.

Others like me seek to appreciate the similarities of all cultures, religions, and ethnicities, as they reach for a higher perception of themselves and the world. Only today I received a book entitled *The Seven Commandments for Happiness and Prosperity*, written by Shari Sharifi Brown, a structural engineer born as a Muslim who converted to Christianity and married into a Jewish-American family. Her deep adherences to all three of the Abrahamic religions help her understand their innate compatibility. Ms. Brown contends that the similarities of the three religions outweigh the differences. I go one step beyond alluding to the similarities of the religions by trusting we are united and aligned to Spirit... We are not alone and are evolving with a universal plan for all of humanity. I call this spirituality and self-development, which are the road to understanding religion and human nature and the only way to higher consciousness.

Ms. Brown wrote, "History has shown us without doubt that we can't depend on political or religious leaders to show us the way. Following Ms. Brown's seven commandments is completely incompatible with their aims of seeking wealth and power. Jewish, Christian, and Muslim leaders sought worldly glory, and to achieve that, they rejected the simple message of their religious founders... We cannot know God. We can only experience God. How do we experience God? First, by believing he is real. Second, by searching for him deep inside ourselves. The way to get in touch is pretty traditional to all religions. There's no other name for it really. It's called prayer."

Spirituality, in my inner thoughts, is the remembering of one's intuition through self-investigation, leading us to transcend ego, mind, or religious belief systems and find the part of our being that is eternal and part of the God Source. Spiritual messages for my clients often help them realize unequivocally the dual nature of their life force and the need to work as one with both.

There are beautiful words, thoughts, songs, and guidance from the energetic place of souls in Spirit if we listen and observe. I feel we are now in a new spiritual awakening and finding this truth is inevitable.

❖

I have been often pleasantly surprised by my spiritual friends and guides and was recently most delighted to have an experience that quite clearly shows how close-by our spiritual friends are standing. During my interview with Doug Heyes, author of *The Touch*, we talked about a patient in the rehab center where Doug was recovering from a serious, debilitating skiing accident. Doug wrote the following story in his book, "I realized that if it is possible for a group of guys to lay their hands on me and transmit this healing energy, why couldn't I do that for someone else? Spirit's voice was soft but clear. 'What makes you think you can't?'"

After hearing that comment in his inner thoughts, Doug returned to the rehab center, and the first person he saw was Pat. "'Pat,' I said, 'Come on. I need a witness.'" Doug and Pat entered Macie's room and positioned themselves on either side of her bed. "Macie," Doug said, "I've been out in the garden again, and God told me he was going to allow me to heal people by putting my hands on them."

"Oh, would you put your hands on me, please?" Macie said.

Doug put his hands-on Macie's legs and began to pray, just as the men on the mountain had prayed for him. Doug prayed that God would be with them and that Macie would be healed.

After a half hour or so, Doug was drained but elated, exhausted, sand pent. The next morning, the first-person Doug saw walking down the hall was Macie. "There he is!" she repeated. "The power of Christ was done, come through Doug, and I can walk again today."

After recording the show, I was saying to Doug that I had hoped to tell the story of Macie during the interview, but it never happened. Doug laughed and responded, "Oh, please, Sheryl. I hope you have a chance to relay this story to your audience, for I truly know who I work for." I replied, "I work for the same God." At that very moment, the lights in my recording room and the computer started to go wild, flashing on and off continuously! Doug and I lost our telephone connection, and an intuitive thought ran through my head: "We thank you both for your diligence, hard work, and conscious recognition of God's desire to love us all with His healing light." I ran upstairs and called Doug from my cell phone. He picked up immediately, laughed, and said he had this light show before!

Holding memories of the joyful, light interactions with other healers like Doug makes it easier for me to engage in situations that are sometimes sad and painful.

Always choosing to find the good and positive in all happenings or simply seeing them as opportunities for needed change, I try to banish negativity and fear as much as possible and to see the silver lining beneath the surface. With that mindset, I embarked on my way to hospice in my usual upbeat manner, creating within myself a calm and beautiful state of peace to bring to others. While parking the car, I saw a dove right in front of me. As this is the message my mom in Spirit always sends, I knew something prophetic might happen. After entering the building, I immediately felt a strong energy field pull me toward a doorway and into a room. Entering that room, I saw a woman lying in bed lifting her arms to the sky, as my mom had done when she was in hospice. The woman, sitting at the side of the bed, told me her mother's name was Carmela. Carmela and my mom were the same age, had alert minds, and looked much younger, though both of them were past 85. Carmela had been ill for some time. The similarities to my own mom's illness and ultimate passing seemed extraordinary.

Carmela's daughter started to cry and told me that her 20-year-old child had just been diagnosed with type 1 diabetes. I felt a flutter in my heart and told her that my son, Gregg had been diagnosed at 22 during the same time my mother was in hospice. I knew quite well the sorrow and anguish this young woman was dealing with, a dying mother and a child who had a difficult challenge before her. We talked about all the positive ways to approach her mother's terminal illness and how her daughter would take care of herself and prosper. I believe we both felt guided and knew there was no challenge that was beyond our capabilities, our spiritually driven life plan, or our love for our children and parents.

In the oneness of being, all of us deal with the loss of parents and children who may be handed an unfair hardship. Yet knowing we are spiritual beings having a physical life might allow us to surrender, trust, and acknowledge that with acceptance and love, we must embrace any happening, for there are no mistakes. We may even find, in time, a precious purpose for what now seems an impossible sadness.

As I left Carmela's daughter's room and wandered into another room to visit another patient, I met a wonderfully alert man. He told me he was 80 years old, and his wife, who had Parkinson's disease, was in the next room in poor condition. The man had osteoporosis and was in pain most of the time. He relayed to me that he and his family had lived through the depression era and had navigated from bad times to good times, and eventually he was able to provide a prosperous, happy life for his family. He told me he was like a sponge and eager to continue to learn, and he attributed much of his success in life to his curious nature. Then he asked me about my work.

When I described energy balancing and healing work, he was most interested. I asked if he would like to relax and breathe in sync with me. I used no touch for this interaction. I thought of an ancient symbol of distant healing, which I often use and which is an integral part of my energy work. I was delighted to share the experience of Reiki with him, and together we sent the intention of healing to his wife in the next room. When he finally opened his eyes, there was such a look of gratitude and knowingness that was quite rewarding to us both.

He thanked me and stated, "You must feel very gratified to share peace through Reiki with so many people." Being the curious fellow, he had always been, he told me when he got home, he would go on his computer to read all about Reiki.

What was unknown becomes known, and then
there is greater truth, hope, or love.

CHAPTER 8
Commitment to Soul Growth

Intention and expectation about outcome guide our reality.
Adam, *The Path of the Dream Healer*

The holiday season has arrived yet again, and while I am always delighted by this magical time of year, celebrating both Chanukah and Christmas, much like other people, I can be overwhelmed by the fast-paced demands of family, work, and friends. Christmas Eve is here, and I am with a friend at St. Agnes Church in Rockville Centre, which brims with beautiful decorations and families beginning their holiday in a reverent way. Once many years ago, I went to St. Agnes and remembered the church as being dimly lit and heavy with incense. This year, the church was well lit. Renovations to the physical building, as well as to rethinking and modernizing practices within the beliefs and policies of the church, as well as other religious denominations, are illuminating souls and might in time bring us to a more personalized unified spiritual way of relating to God. It seems time to go beyond fundamental restrictive thinking to seek a higher consciousness and personal connection to God, to the light and beauty of mankind's evolution. These thoughts were very apparent to me on this special night. Evolution leads us towards justice, love, and harmony. Though I do not consider myself bound by religious rules, I do consider myself a child of the Universe and eternal love, and as an adult, I feel comfortable with people who worship or seek knowledge in many ways.

Of course, the beautiful music filled my heart essence, and I felt that many of the people present in this sacred church realized the actual meaning of Christmas. Christmas was a gathering and sharing of loving intentions expressed in words read that shared the eternal message of Jesus and songs sung that filled the large building with a powerful resonance and strength. This made the experience very poignant. It seemed to me that many people view Jesus as the symbol of the lamb, representing the spirit and soul of God and the peace offered so generously.

The lion obviously represents the physical complications of the body and physical life. The body knows only its endless need to feel safe and to survive, restricting it from embracing the higher realm of God in Spirit. To me, Spirit is limitless, endless, and has the capacity to share love in its purest form. Therefore, the soul only wishes to interact with others to create peace and emit love. Hearing the voice of one's soul is an awakening of higher consciousness that gives us the freedom to conquer the physical world and live in God's love.

One need not die physically to experience this freedom. One must simply seek to hear the voice of reason that says, "I am eternal. I wish to quiet the thoughts and fears of mind and ego to hear the voice and guidance of Spirit. As I resonate and feel with my heart, I touch my soul. This higher consciousness or feeling of connectedness is much wiser than my intellect."

After I felt these beautiful thoughts within my heart, a priest began to speak, and it felt like he was speaking to me personally. There were hundreds of people in this well-packed, large, auspicious church. The priest told a story of walking into a church years before and observing what was engraved in wood above the church door. It read, "Enter at your own risk." I was amused, for I had discovered entering the church or any spiritual pursuit meant a closer connection with spirit, more intimate and more binding, and one is forever changed!

When one commits to that deeper connection
or relationship, change is inevitable.

❖

Since most people fear change, they resist commitment to their soul growth or development. They linger in a state of physical unconsciousness. It is easier to feed the physical body than it is to feed your spiritual essence. There can be little change in a person's understanding of who they are when they are only concerned with the joys of a physical life. I believe that we are all entitled to a beautiful and joyful material life, but it will not happen fully if we only focus to that end and the spiritual concerns and issues of a person are denied.

When one aspires to love their essence and entire being, physical and energetic, major changes in all aspects of life must occur.

❖

Change begins subtly. The Universe rewards progress with little surprises and miracles. Little messages from above in the form of coincidences or delightful occurrences bring smiles and pleasure to me and others on a daily basis. I have learned to be open to small miracles and to know that those who seek to give more than they take are often happier. This is Newton's Third Law which says, "For every action, there is an equal and opposite reaction."

Events that transpired over the next few days allowed holiday synchronicities and Newton's Law to present itself abundantly during the holiday season. I went into one of my favorite Italian restaurants and was handed two quarters and a dime at the counter. I went to put the money in my pocket. The dime dropped.

As I stopped to pick it up, three dimes dropped to the floor. I picked them up. The woman next to me said, "You must have a hole in your pocket." I reached into my pocket, and four quarters came out where I had only two before. No hole there. Then another dime fell out. I went to pick it up as more dimes fell. Now, I had seven dimes and four quarters. "Where are the dimes coming from?" the woman asked.

"I don't know. Perhaps, it's like that movie, *It's a Wonderful Life.* Do you know that movie?"

"Yes!" she responded. Perhaps such little miracles or acknowledgements are from God and his helpers to lighten and brighten our days. Perhaps this incident was a message from my mom as the sequenced numbers eleven and seven designated the month and day she died and also the day she crossed over into a new spiritual life. Perhaps she wanted to say hello or just amuse me. The coins dropping quite simply out of the air might have been Spirit's way of reminding me that the main character, George, in *It's a Wonderful Life* thought he had missed out on life and was a failure because he hadn't made a lot of money. In reality, the angel, Clarence, showed George that if he had not lived, hundreds of people would have suffered, died, and been worse off. George's acceptance of his life plan to remain in a small town, serve the people, and forgo his dream to travel and have exotic experiences aligned to his higher nature of goodness, hard work, and resilience and were in fact, what made a most wonderful life.

Linda Deir, author of *Guided* and a recent guest on *Healing from Within*, like many who have been on my show, is another example of someone able to clarify and refine her own needs for understanding and enjoying life. In her book, Linda shares her journey of transformation and her search into the metaphysical realms that began in her childhood. Linda struggled to answer childhood questions such as, "Why does my mother dislike me and make me suffer?" and "Why am I struggling to survive this childhood?" Linda goes on to tell me the only reason she survived the brutal beatings and emotional torment was because she was able to speak to angels or souls from the afterlife whom she knew had her best interests at heart and loved her unconditionally. Higher souls taught Linda about the principles of energy. Through her own thoughts, she discovered she would be able to engage in positive, life-affirming behaviors or succumb to the negative conditions of her family life. The choice, even as a child, was hers. Linda's guides told her that if she could simply make it through childhood, life would improve and she would find joy and happiness. These spiritual entities that guided Linda taught her everything of value for becoming an honest and truthful person, helping her develop an ability to discern whether people in her life could be relied on or not relied on. Ultimately, we learn from Linda's story that holding onto hope, faith, and trust are the keys to transcending early traumatic conditions. In Linda's case, her salvation came from her ability to trust these spiritual protectors.

We often find that the most auspicious events or challenges lead us to find ourselves and the great gift of life in all its forms in the Universe. Therefore, the power to survive and thrive is indeed within our own being.

CHAPTER 9
Becoming Conscientious Citizens

Trust thyself: every heart vibrates to that iron string. Accept the place the divine providence has found for you, the society of your contemporaries, the connection of events. Great men have always done so…
Ralph Waldo Emerson

Messages and stories received for my clients during meditation help me recognize that a multitude of small pleasures is provided by our loved ones and guides in Spirit who wish us to have pleasure in life. While there may be events that cause suffering, suffering need not be embraced or encouraged, and we must move toward joy and happiness, as that is our natural state of being. Information from Spirit offers us ways to appreciate personal abilities and preferences and gain greater respect for the uniqueness of our personality. That awareness allows us to find a way to accept everything and everyone, without a concept of good vs. bad or right vs. wrong, helping us to eliminate many unproductive opinions or biases and allowing the objective part of our soul to observe the bigger picture and remain neutral and unbiased so we may create our own interactive story with the world of our emotions.

Having a physical life is truly a gift. I believe not every soul in the Universe has this opportunity.

❖

As higher vibrational beings, therefore souls of positive energy, we eventually may come to know we are not alone and miraculously possessing the gift of divine love and self-awareness.

Only recently, another wonderful moment and message were delivered from my mother-in-spirit when I spent the day with my two-year-old granddaughter, Samantha. At the end of the day, I had difficulty getting her bracelet off. All of a sudden, she said, "Oh, man!" I laughed because that was my mother's pet phrase and Samantha had the exact tone and expression. It was almost as if my mom was in the room! Then I got Samantha into her pajamas, and she jumped up and down, saying, "I am so happy."

"Why are you so happy today?"

"Because Grandmama, you came to see me today." So much love expressed by a little child, but the depth and wisdom of her soul are eons beyond her physical presence.

Dimitri Moraitis, coauthor of *Change Your Aura Change Your Life*, writes, "As a parent, it is important to recognize that your child is a full, complete soul with free will and a destiny all its own... Parents may look at the child and think it's so cute and helpless, but connected to that child is a full adult soul slowly establishing itself. Although parents are responsible for the child's upbringing, they are not responsible for that child's evolution. The soul within the child is responsible for its own spiritual development."

This moment with Samantha was a reflection of love and soul life that I had with my mother while she was alive and now with her in Spirit. It also stimulated a feeling that made me think, "Whatever did I do to receive such a moment of grace and sheer enjoyment?" It would seem love is often expressed in a single moment by a simple action, word, glance, or song of the heart, as well as momentous spiritual events like the one I experienced the night before my father died.

The night before my father died, I was lying in bed sick with the flu when quite suddenly, I felt a shadow or presence at my right side and *knew* it was my grandfather William. He projected a thought in my mind... "You have to write something for your father." I woke up very confused. The next day, still sick in bed, I received a phone call from my mom telling me my dad had died. He had been frail for years, but still, hearing he had passed was a shock. This event would not be understood until many years later when I would discover the truth of who I am...who we all are. We are all beings of divine energy and physical possibilities at the same time.

Ultimately, this discovery has helped me to accept the loss of my father and other loved ones, as I know we will all be reunited beyond life.

People involved in the study of metaphysics, psychology, quantum physics, and energy healing help others discover the truth about their soul longevity, allowing them to remember the eternal unbroken chain of life here and in Spirit. We do not have to wait to be beyond our physical life to realize the enormity of our soul's ability to bridge the gap between the two worlds of finite and infinite being. We are part of the endless circle of life.

In ancient cultures before traditional concepts of medicine as practiced by today's medical community, the care and spiritual needs of the community were attended to by shamans. Shamans were the protectors of the mind, body, and spiritual needs of the village and as such, had their feet in two worlds or were the bridge between the seen and unseen worlds. In interviewing wonderful authors and modern-day shamans, we are able to see that the ancient philosophy and wisdom of the Mexican Toltec culture are still appropriate for healing on a personal and collective level. Shamanism teaches us that everything that exists is alive and has a spirit. Shamans speak of a "web of life" that connects all of life and the Spirit or Divine that lives in all things. Everything on Earth is interconnected, and any belief that we are separate from other life forms, including the Earth, stars, wind, and so on, is an illusion. In view of this description, I have come to recognize that we are all shamans for creative change, transforming ourselves and the world into the most refined condition as we awaken to the fact that we are more than our physical life. Seeking the creative force within allows us to enjoy beauty, warmth, love, and kindness while appreciating nature and our sensory connection to the breath of life. It is through the processes of art, music, poetry, writing, singing, and vibrational music that we draw in God's compassion and express it into the physical world. It would be advantageous for every person to seek that connection of mind, body, and spirit in order to share the best of this God-like vigor connecting us with the inspiration of the Universe. Shamans assist us in expressing our thoughts and actions, enabling us to reach the deeper part of our divine expression, bridging the worlds of the known and unknown.

❖

Relationships

It seems to me that close to New Year's, there are often synchronistic meetings between people from the past. It's almost as if the Universe wants to have us renew and review our connections to each other and reinforce our direction in the New Year. In my case, this New Year presented moments of grace, providing me with support and much love. It appears the support I hope to share with others was being returned to me.

The basis for all relationships should be love,
affection, and mutual respect.

❖

Commitment to help friendships or to encourage love to grow over time is also necessary. This would be true of any interaction between people who have a continuous connection. This would include siblings, married partners, business associates, and friends. It also appears that a certain segment of our population that includes caretakers and people involved in spiritual enterprises, such as teachers, health practitioners, and parents, indeed nurturing people, often tend to give much more than they expect to receive. They are almost always embarrassed when given gifts or attention, as they are more inclined to be givers than takers. It is in their nature.

People who are seen as takers seem to be demanding, often feeling entitled to have everything, and are very self-absorbed. They often disregard others and are oblivious to their own insensitive actions, which is a sadness to observe. Partially acting from their ego or physical sense differentiates them from people acting from their true soul essence, who can only think of others first. It is this condition that seems to be so prevalent in our modern-day governing officials. Have they lost their connection to Spirit?

All of these continuing observations cannot be accomplished without an understanding of Universal energy. The divine energy that flows around us and within us is the source of all intuition and inspirational wisdom, and it is this help from above that allows us to transform our emotions and our physical life and to know truth.

In ancient societies, the Greeks, Romans, Native American Indians, and others found ways of utilizing this Universal energy for releasing negativity and tensions from their physical body. They followed spiritual practices to attain higher consciousness, hoping for peace and survival. Physical health and emotional well-being were their primary needs and were supplied through simplistic and holistic ways of interacting with the physical world. At the same time, ancient cultures used all forms of beautification of the physical body and elevated consciousness by exercise, meditation, music, art, theater, and dance. In other words, speaking to the soul through beauty and creativity, instead of the mundane and primitive baseness of slovenly life, were ordinary practices for survival.

More people are reawakening to these useful yet spiritually charged art forms. By merging physical needs with spiritual energy forces, like-minded people and organizations will begin to form stronger foundations for opening the doorway to higher thought, possibilities, and a more wholesome, refined view and presentation of life. We will eventually all become conscientious citizens of the larger cosmos.

Before we can become aware of ourselves as spiritual beings of eternal energy, we must master the physical, emotional, intellectual, and instinctual boundaries of our human life.

❖

Karma

The law of karma, or cause-and-effect, that states each action brings an equal reaction, is always in effect. Having a positive intention often brings many pleasant experiences, while focusing on one's own agenda for personal gain at the expense of others often brings trauma, drama, and unwanted responses in the form of health challenges, financial mishaps, or loss of life and limb. As it is often said, "What goes around comes around." Sometimes actions happen repeatedly over time, but ultimately karma will be satisfied, and what one sows, one will reap.

I went to McDonald's recently for a cup of tea. A young, dark-haired Hispanic man with a dimpled, kind smile and physical warmth and beauty said "Hello." He asked if I remembered him, and I said, "You used to be at the bagel store near my office. Your name is Miguel."

When I went to pay for my tea, the cashier said it was paid for. I proceeded to the pickup window, where Miguel said, "I am taking care of it...A gift for the holidays." Miguel also handed me my favorite chocolate-chip cookies. What a gracious, unexpected gift. I thanked Miguel and left with a big smile on my face. Did he feel the energy of a soul connection from a past life? Or was it the thought from his soul essence to treat another person kindly? Unity and love come from breaking down boundaries and remembering we are all connected through time and space and through the oneness of our souls. Learning to release this force for goodness must be the impetus in all our enterprises. When you are in this higher state of receiving energy from above and dispersing it without expectation, then the best of everything can be returned to you. The Law of Attraction is always at work. If you function at this level on a regular basis, you will tend to have more prosperity, health, and joy.

To feel your true energy or being allows you to
connect to others by giving freely.

❖

I was reminded of how I felt when my friend Gloria moved to Florida a few years ago. People were always moving, and like most people, adjusting to change was sometimes hard for me. The next day I received Gloria's Christmas card in the mail. The scene on the card showed snow adorned with glitter amongst a long row of trees in the forest. The forest seemed empty, silent, and beautiful under the night sky. Gloria's card relayed a message much like a blessing, sharing words of wisdom and hope from a friend of years ago. Though we rarely speak, Gloria encourages me to my highest sense of purpose. I reminded myself to call her. Later that day, I met two women named Gloria, and I knew the Universe was telling me to make a phone call. I immediately called Gloria and left a message.

The day after Christmas, I went into a local store in Woodbury. My phone rang. Often, I don't get a message or even hear my phone ring, but this call came through immediately. I retrieved it and heard Gloria's voice. She was here in New York at her daughter's house, 15 minutes away from me. We met at a local restaurant, where we enjoyed our reunion, uplifting for both of us.

We discussed how we had no choice but to continue on our path in search of divine wisdom, guidance, and maintaining our high energy level and our service to Spirit. We talked of our relationships to people in our lives and about finding ways to harness joy and peace and acknowledged how grateful and blessed we are.

Gloria has had two divorces, and was a woman of deep spiritual objective. Gloria had difficulty finding a partner who shared her strong intentions and beliefs. Yet, she had not relinquished her need for personal soul growth for a relationship. I think that is what it means to be true to oneself, even when it might mean walking alone. We all wish to love and be loved, but in Gloria's search for her Higher Self, she continued to seek an equal partner capable of an authentic or sacred relationship, even though this is not an easy pursuit. Spiritually aware individuals like Gloria are on a quest to find and build commitment to love through trust, honesty, and their own continued soul refinement. Holding true to her highest soul goals and destiny often required extreme sacrifices and adjustments.

Nothing and no one are ever lost. We merely need to include new experiences and friends into our life journey.

CHAPTER 10
Marriages Arranged In Heaven

*In everyone's life at some time, our inner fire goes out. It is then
burst into flames by an encounter with another human being.
We should all be thankful for those people who rekindle inner spirit.*
Albert Schweitzer

My plane flew out of Kennedy Airport for Miami, where I was to embark
on a five-day cruise to the Bahamas hosted by my yoga teacher, Pam
Rudderman. I greatly appreciated her talent and efforts and was happy to
join her and some other participants in the yoga class I attended. While I
waited to embark the ship and go to my stateroom, the steward directed
me to the café lounge for lunch. The lounge was teaming with people, and
I saw an empty chair at a table where two women and a young child were
seated and walked over to ask if I could sit in one of the chairs.

It didn't take me long to find out that the young woman, Lea, was a
cardiac nurse from Toronto. My son had just married another Lea from
California, also a cardiac nurse at the time. Since then, Lea has become a
Nurse Practitioner. The young woman's daughter, Megan, couldn't wait to
get to the swimming pool. I mentioned to them how I often meet people
from Canada and England and have visited and enjoyed both places.

Lea and Megan left, and a gentleman approached the table and asked
in an elegant and refined English accent if he might sit at the table. His
wife soon joined him, and I could feel it was the second marriage for both.
Their names were Amy and Richard. They lived in New Jersey and owned
a house in Montauk on Long Island. I observed both to be tall, energetic,
and well-matched in physical appearance and energy. Amy asked if I was
a medium, perhaps noticing I was so observant or because she herself was
spiritually gifted. I explained my work as an intuitive energy healer and
medium. She asked for my card and said she had heard of me.

Amy, a true believer that everything happens for a reason, had her own stories to support this. It immediately became clear to me that my meeting with Amy and Richard would have an unusual twist of fate. They both worked for different companies in different countries that held national conventions in Japan, where Richard, from England, and Amy, from the U.S., first met. A long-distance working relationship led to better conditions for the companies they worked for and eventually their marriage, even though there were challenges in a long-distance romance. True synchronicity is the fact that they met at all and soon found they shared an amazing connection.

Amy told me an unusual coincidence. Her father was in the Italian Army during World War II and was taken prisoner in Ethiopia before he was sent to a farm prison in England. Richard's father ran that prison facility, and the two fathers knew each other well. Both had recently passed and were in spirit, and Amy and I entertained the idea that perhaps their fathers had orchestrated the events that led to Amy and Richard's meeting. It seemed that cooperation between the two men, both in life and in Spirit, possibly helped create a fulfilling and better destiny for their children.

I showed them a picture of my son, Gregg, and Lea, who had just married on June 21st. Funny, but Lea was a California girl who went to New York to work, and Gregg, a New Yorker, left to work in San Francisco. Several years before, I had been told by a medium that my dad-in-spirit was arranging for a very special girl for Gregg. This special girl lived on a different coast, but destiny soon brought them together. Lea broke off an engagement in New York, returned to California, and rented an apartment in Gregg's building in San Francisco. Both were interested in other potential mates. However, their destiny was to eventually find each other.

I believe, or wish to believe, in divine intervention and that they had help from the spiritual realm.

❖

Thinking back to my plane ride to Florida for this Bahamian cruise, I had shown the woman sitting next to me a picture of Gregg and Lea, now my daughter-in-law, as I am so happy to see my children in loving relationships.

"Oh," she said, "Lea is not Jewish, I gather." I couldn't understand how she could determine this by looking at a picture.

"No, she is not Jewish," I responded, "and I couldn't be happier with Gregg's choice."

As a spiritual healer, I have been granted the gift to see past issues of religion, race, and gender to find the more energetic component of each soul and connect with people seeing the beauty within—or the lack of it.

"Religion is important to me, and I'm sorry she's not Jewish," the young woman continued.

"Beyond this physical life," I responded, "One is not a Jew, a Catholic, a Muslim, not black, white, Asian, or Indian. One is a soul connected to God and each other in pure energy and love. Religion often creates separation and divisiveness, making people unable to appreciate the inner qualities that belong to us all."

As Mahatma Gandhi said, "God has no religion."

❖

When people can be present, awaken to the knowledge of their own soul, and connect through prayer or meditation to God, they become aware without any religious training or man-made belief systems that they can be at peace and at one with the dynamic Universe. Belonging to a temple or church and learning the doctrines do not ensure that one truly is living and practicing God's highest dictates. I believe when you love and accept yourself or others without judgment or fear, you are able to connect to each other in friendship and brotherhood. You honor God.

When I related this story to Amy and Richard, Amy said she was Catholic and had been married to an Orthodox Rabbi. She had converted to Judaism. She felt that the woman who had responded in the way she did on the plane had limited exposure to other religions and perhaps spoke out of ignorance. It did not upset Amy or me to realize that some people, but not all, are so attached to their systematic, cultural, and religious beliefs that they are unable to climb to a higher state of spirituality that seeks a personal, heartfelt, intimate connection to God, although we feel it would be a perfect time for a shift away from this limited thinking by members of any religious persuasion.

The greatest freedom is to attain liberation from society's rules,
beliefs, and mores to find the truth of who you really are beyond
the labels and identification of our physical standards.
When you connect to the heart of a person's
being, it is beyond human limitation.

CHAPTER 11
Merging Mind and Heart
for Heaven on Earth

Non-resistance, non-judgment, and nonattachment are the
three aspects of true freedom and enlightened living.
Eckhart Tolle, *A New Earth*

As always, I cannot fail to notice Spirit's way of making me smile by once again reminding me that we are not alone and that Spirit means to uplift and better our condition. This thought became exceedingly clear to me recently when I was at my Lexus dealership having my car serviced. When I went to get a bagel in the waiting area, a woman named Esther was standing next to me, attempting to make a cup of coffee in the sophisticated, modern coffee machine.

I commented that a new coffee machine, a Keurig, that makes one cup at a time was just brought into the building where I have my office. We all enjoyed the simplicity of that machine. Brian Katz had brought the machine to the building for everyone to share and enjoy and was perhaps trying to make the ordinary workplace more comfortable for himself and others, maybe to create a magical, joyful environment.

When people share a cup of coffee, they share a love for the finer things in life, like the enjoyment of ordinary friendship, cooperation, and coordinated efforts to succeed, and life is then lighter and more meaningful. It's like the golden rule of loving thy neighbor as you love thyself. I helped Esther make the cup of coffee, and then she sat down next to me. It soon became apparent to both of us that we were placed together to validate each other's spiritual truths.

Esther had lost her husband recently. He was 55 years old. She was a special-education teacher in the New York City schools, as I had been only a few years ago. I told her about my book *The Living Spirit* and my belief that our loved ones are only a hop and a skip away from us. Esther also mentioned that she had a dear friend, also a teacher, who practiced Reiki and now lived in New Jersey. She told me her friend was hoping she might move closer to her, and I sensed that this was a strong possibility.

Sometimes when one relationship ends, we are able to find new experiences to further open our hearts to a new and different kind of love. No loss, in my opinion, is a punishment, but just a necessary change for everyone concerned to grow and gain greater perceptions of their own magnificent soul potential and their eternal nature.

Most of us do not like change, but it is impossible to stop time, space in physical reality, and the evolution of our energetic, spiritual nature. Change we will, and change we must. Embracing everyone and every event, some quite difficult, is our ticket to the future.

A few tears dropped from Esther's eyes as we both realized divine intervention had placed us side by side. The spirit of a smile danced on my lips as I realized it was another wonderful, miraculous coincidence.

The conquering of ordinary fears and attachments to this world and to people, which are only temporary, is the outcome of your awakening. I believe it is God's greatest plan and intention for all of us to eventually have this grand awakening.

❖

My youngest granddaughter, Talia Eve, shared a poem she wrote the other day that shows me that even a child as young as seven years old grapples with understanding her physical life needs as well as the responsibilities of her soul and heart.

Talia wrote:

"In my heart, I close my eyes, begging my heart to go to sleep, but it can't hear me because it's already asleep in its own way.

So, I close my eyes once more, and I dream of marvelous things that can't happen in a regular life because magic makes it happen."

The magic is the remembrance and trust in the soul to know life is not ordinary but extraordinary.

❖

Awakening

Since becoming conscious of energies or life that surround us all, I am also aware that a greater awakening is happening to many individuals, communities, nations, and the world at large. This awareness allows for a clearer view of humanity and our spiritual condition and could bring together all the diverse religions for honoring God together. The combined forces of God and humanity merging beliefs, traditions, and the many cultural and racial values can bring about the ultimate holistic healing of our world. If we could take the knowingness of our total life force and unite within our minds and hearts, the world would truly reflect heaven on earth. As science has improved the quality of physical life, it is now possible for us to be become more intelligent, more wholesome, more tolerant, and healthier beings so we can live longer lives with greater compassion, understanding, and love.

To accomplish this, one must conquer the negativity and fear the ego mind inflicts. Unabashedly fear restricts us from connecting to other people. We must not see others as threats, but as like us in all ways, just fragile humans subject to moments of confusion, doubt, poor choices, and mistakes. In the end, each person wishes to return to that inner call to be both at peace and to have success in this physical life. I believe the political unrest that rages across our world right now is part of God's plan in this grand spiritual evolution, and once past the chaos and divisiveness, we will find our way to a new respect for each other and life.

I am reminded that the former Pope Benedict XVI visited Yankee Stadium years ago and spoke to over 50,000 people in Yankee Stadium. Prior to that stop, he visited a Jewish synagogue where Passover was being observed. The awareness of the connection to God by the Hebrews, who were the first to believe in an invisible God of Spirit 4000 years ago, is observed between the three Abrahamic religions: Judaism, Christianity, and Islam. Observations of the energetic condition of God can transform traditions and beliefs to a higher spiritual truth. It is time for the leaders of different religions to reach within their own divine souls, move beyond the books and traditions of past times, and embrace the love of all who honor the Divine personally and collectively without differentiation.

When God spoke to the Israelites and called them His chosen people for believing in Him and the loving power of His energy, perhaps, He meant that all the people on Earth who act in good faith are His chosen people. At the end of our physical lives, we will return to a dimension of higher thought and pure energetic life and share a less physical experience than we have become accustomed to as humans, but we will carry with us the remembrances of being human.

This type of love is known as Universal love. Before we know it, the world will have evolved to a new level of being, as so many people are taking a giant leap into a consciousness that channels God's overwhelming love at all times.

❖

It is only with the heart that one can see rightly; what is essential is invisible to the eye.
Antoine de Saint-Exupery, 1900-1944 French Aviator and Writer
The Little Prince

I arrived at Miami Airport after returning from the Bahamian cruise, boarded my plane, and headed back home to La Guardia Airport in New York. We were seated, and the pilot announced that the plane had been delayed, as weather conditions in New York had backed up all flights. There was no telling how long we would have to sit in our seats.

The woman next to me, Phyllis, had the outside seat but had let the man in the middle seat go sit with his wife. Another young man with a terrible cold took the outside seat. Phyllis was now in the middle, and I was by the window. She was not happy to have someone with a bad cold sitting next to her. She had been happy to help the other man but had not expected this scenario.

I wanted to comfort her in some small way, so I told her I was a Reiki intuitive healer and would send the intention and energy for us to do well on the flight and to remain healthy.

Phyllis mentioned she had lost her son several years ago. He was only 32 years old and the father of three young children. Her friends had arranged for her to have a telephone reading with a psychic medium of world renown. She felt she had not heard what she needed to assure her that her son was all right. I told her in my first experience with a spiritual reading by a medium, I was also skeptical. Yet what was told to me made sense over time.

Phyllis was hurt and skeptical and thought all things in life were random. I told her about my book *Life Is No Coincidence* and my belief that nothing is random. Once I had been as skeptical and also believed life was just a throw of the dice. I thought everything could be explained scientifically by using logic and intellect. Now, as a result of personal experiences and years of training and experience working with the unseen force of energy, I knew that much can only be felt and not seen.

She challenged me to do a reading for her to prove that there was truth to my words. Wanting to help her, I took the dare. She handed me a pen and pad. I closed my eyes, grounded myself, and meditated. I asked Spirit for messages that would help this woman go forward in her own spiritual healing and help her release her pain and sadness.

I received some appropriate information about her physical being and her relationship with her second husband from her father in Spirit. All the messages were right on the money. I sensed that perhaps when she had had the reading with the other medium, she was not willing or able to understand why her son had died and was closed down or not ready to hear from him. Perhaps it was not the time for her son to communicate with her. If one wishes to be given and shown all the truths of the Universe but is not receptive, no one can help them.

Whether my messages were poignant enough to change her perception and bring back a sense of peace and a release of her sadness about losing her only son, I cannot be sure. I did the best I could under the circumstances.

Doing Readings

It is becoming clearer to me that it doesn't matter where I am when I am called to do a reading. I always thought I had to work in my office or in a room where I had established a higher peaceful energy. I know now that I must be available when the situation calls for me to connect both to the person who asks for help and the souls above who send it. That is part of the responsibility of this type of energy work.

I believe Spirit gives messages that a person might be able to handle at the present time. No more and nothing less seems to be given. There I was, high above in the rainy skies, doing a reading. Most mediums are paid well for their services, but I was asked, and I responded without hesitation because another human being had asked. At that moment, I was not a businesswoman, just a conscious being entrusted with gifts to use, no matter what the time, place, or occasion. Phyllis did, however, treat me to a drink.

CHAPTER 12
To Reach for Higher Ground

Give me beauty in the inward soul; may the
outward and the inward man be at one.
Socrates, c470 - 399 BC

Over the course of my working life, David and others have observed me take on many responsibilities and work hard as a teacher, a manager of a furniture showroom, and a businesswoman. In these roles, success was determined in visual ways such as a paycheck. Now, some people felt that my fascination about unbounded ways for the human imagination to reach beyond the normal boundaries of a physical presence is a waste of time. They cannot see the purpose of exploring unseen energy patterns, which could offer immense ways for transforming people's thoughts, enabling them to find happiness, well-being, and a sense of their true purpose in life.

Clients who have experienced energy-healing sessions have begun to understand themselves, their relationships, and their goals and desires. Many have been helped to bring about major shifts in their awareness of their self, becoming more aware of their bodies and the formless soul. Knowing their soul more deeply often allows for forgiveness, for endless hurt and pain to be released, and for ways to embrace a new future.

It seems my true destiny after all my other earlier life experiences was to reawaken my soul talent to communicate with Spirit and serve. The exchange of money required for being in alignment to Universal Source is inconsequential and doing what you do best is the important aspect of this process.

All life love valued by Spirit is necessary for the evolution of all souls.
Acceptance of oneself is the major key to new perceptions
and thoughts that bring about new realities.

❖

Recently, a 20-year-old man came to me for his first session. He was discharged from the army and told me he had bipolar disorder. In my observation, most people are functioning with some form of physical or emotional disorder. The young man told me he came from a family with rampant alcoholism and drug abuse, which, as we all know, are major problems in society today. We are a world in pain. Perhaps we are a world that has lost all connection to the energy and love that are our natural soul birthright. It seems healing may only begin when we discover our soul and open to the voice within.

My client told me that last month he tried to commit suicide. All he really wanted was to feel safe and happy again, and he knew he needed help. I expressed to him that I believed we were all born with a plan and a set of circumstances to work with. In order to discover our plan and purpose in life, we have to find and begin to express the greatest good and love that reside within us. To do that, we must realize that our suffering is often self-induced by thinking of the worst scenario that could befall us instead of concentrating on the good that is always possible.

Moving through difficult, untenable challenges by remaining calm and trusting of love within and all around us and reaching out for help may be ways to remain whole and stable no matter how hard the situation appears to be.

The young man climbed onto my healing table, lying face up with his eyes closed. I played a beautiful, healing CD written for the Dalai Lama. His body relaxed, and he asked me, "What do you feel, Sheryl?" I told him I felt no serious physical pain and he was healing from the sadness of his past experiences. After the session, I handed him a small packet of cards that have little sayings. Whenever I offer these to a client, the message on the card they pick seems appropriate to the needs of the healing session, offering a helpful clue for a positive approach to the situation. His card read: "How do you know you haven't completed your life's mission? If you're still alive, you haven't." We were both amazed at how appropriate the message was. Before he left, I asked him what message he had received that he liked the best. He responded, "I am supposed to live."

Children & Positive Energy

In my office building children come for training sessions with the physical and occupational therapists. I have watched as children move towards certain people and experiences or shy away from them. Most children are drawn to people of higher positive energy and repelled by negative energy except if they are only exposed to negative energy and must become used to it to survive, as it may be all they know. Colors displayed in the aura or electro-magnetic field of energy around all of us are often seen by some children, and they may be attracted to the brighter, lighter feelings emanating from happy, healthy people who give off this radiance of beautiful, clear, bright colors. The aura reflects the spiritual content and soul aspects of each individual. I am often amused at how the children find their way into my room and have quite open-hearted talks with me. Children are imbued with their own soul awareness and when treated respectfully with kindness, fairness, and love, respond in quite mature ways.

I believe children must be honored and listened to, especially when they express fear or discomfort in any situation. Some adults will say, "They are just children," and then continue to expose them to people and places that frighten them or make them feel uncomfortable. As parents, teachers, and professional healers, we must be aware of children's reactions and intuit the message they are offering, always honoring them with positive reinforcement and praise.

I think back to when Samantha, my first granddaughter, was only three and was energetic, quick, and fast on her feet. She spoke fluently for a three-year-old, just like her mother had as a young child, and Samantha had at times rejected Reiki, and when she did, I respected her wishes. One time when she was sick and feverish, she allowed me to use Reiki to help her. Immediately after the energy-work, she threw up, but then her recovery was rapid. Yesterday, she showed me her arm. She had taken a blood test. I asked if she wanted Reiki, and she nodded yes. I asked if she could feel the energy, and where she felt it? Samantha said she felt it in her heart and it was good. "Will it still hurt me tomorrow?" Samantha asked. I responded that it would be much better by then. I knew that Reiki would help it to heal faster.

My younger granddaughter, Alea Hope, put her hand up to mine at that moment to feel the exchange of energy, and she smiled. She is quite observant and quietly whispered, "I love you." Children instinctively feel and accept Reiki and other healing energies. They are vessels of pure potential until filled with any negative thoughts or fears. Energy awareness and training could help parents and teachers understand their children and help them interact more favorably in the world.

We are the sum total of our experiences and our predispositions through genetic coding. It is my understanding that before a soul incarnates into a physical realm, they select the family, gender, and circumstances that will surround them in order for their soul to rethink, refine, or reprogram their essence so they may rise up to a higher version of themselves. Physical ailments exhibited by members of your family are not automatically going to surface in your life and may or may not have to be experienced by you unless necessary for your soul needs.

I am thinking back to a story I remember from my hospice visits about a grandfather and his twin grandsons who all passed from pancreatic cancer. So it might be a genetic predisposition but also a selection of that soul to be in that family and perhaps experience the same disease as other family members, which may alter a karmic pattern from past-life experiences that ultimately free that soul and family, bringing them forward into the afterlife in an improved version of soul needs.

The next time I went to hospice, I waited to be directed by the nurses, doctors, or staff to someone who might benefit from a volunteer's visit. Walking down the hallway, I saw a tall, young man and a man who was seated in a wheelchair and hooked up to an IV. They were outside on the sun porch. I was so sad to think that a person so young was about to lose a father. I wanted to talk to them in a quiet way, but I felt I might intrude on a special moment they were sharing. I did not go to join them.

Sometime later, Sabrina, a delightful and spiritually joyful nurse, directed me to a room where she thought I could be of service. I entered the room and saw the two men I had seen on the sun porch. The timing was better now for us to meet. The young man was holding a guitar, and I commented that my young granddaughter had just asked for a guitar for her birthday present, and I needed someone to teach her to play.

"I will teach her," he responded genuinely and told me his name was Michael. It was so wonderful to hear him reach out with life and music to a stranger, even as he watched his uncle—not his father I soon discovered—battle a disease that would ultimately take his life.

Michael played some music for us. I told him how beautiful it was to see how close he was to his uncle, who quietly responded, "I love him." When I said what a nice young man he was, the patient told me he didn't have any children of his own, but still he had taken part in this young man's development and growth. He asked his nephew to go and get us some ice cream. To do that, he must take the car and drive a short distance to a supermarket. I sensed he might want to talk to me alone.

The uncle shared with me that he had helped people over the years who were sick or dying, as I was doing. He was aware that more existed beyond this life, but his brother didn't seem to get it and wanted him home when it was his time for him to expire. He didn't want the children to see that. I asked if he felt safe in this place, and he said "Yes." I said, "There are indeed so many caring people around you here at hospice, and they will help you manage the pain." He seemed to agree, and then he asked, "Is your husband alive?"

"Yes," I responded.

"There is a man behind you to guard you." I thanked him for telling me and replied, "As I am an energy healer and medium, I believe as you do, that our energy or Spirit lives after this physical life." I also should have asked him to describe the man. I often wonder whom he saw at that moment.

I could see he was getting tired, so I suggested we both close our eyes and just breathe. When I closed my eyes, I saw a man diving for pearls, and I asked the man if he liked to sell pearls in his jewelry store.

"Yes, I sold pearls, but I had a friend who worked in the booth next to me in Manhattan, and pearls were her specialty." He said, "Pearls are more complex than most people know." I told him that my mother, Ceil, had also loved pearls.

When his nephew returned with the ice cream, the patient offered me one. The patient ate two and drank some juice. This man who was so weak was gracious enough to think of me though he was close to the end of his own life. I told him how grateful I was to have spent time with him and that I would look in on him again, though I knew that his time was short and I might not visit with him again. He threw me a kiss with his hand as I left. I wished him a blissful rest.

Beautiful connections to people of all ages
and walks of life keep happening.
They are validations of Spirit bringing us together meaningfully.

CHAPTER 13
To Teach Is to Touch

Take the first step in faith. You don't have to see
the whole staircase. Just take the first step.
Dr. Martin Luther King Jr.

At hospice today, I was sent to see a woman who was a teacher and had been suffering with multiple sclerosis for years. As a former teacher, I knew the amount of energy and preparation that went into teaching at any grade level. I was aware also that this woman had to have had tremendous willpower to overcome her challenged, sick body to continue teaching for as long as she did.

As I entered the room, she called out, "Sarah, how nice of you to come to see me." I told her my name was Sheryl and I was named for both my grandmothers, who were named Sarah. She responded her granddaughter was Sarah.

In the course of conversation, I mentioned I practiced Reiki energy healing, and she said she had a friend who helped her tremendously over the last five years by administering Reiki to her. She then showed me a handmade blanket, a gift from the other teachers made especially for her retirement. It read, "To teach is to touch."

People who reach out to others and see past gender, job, religion, education, and marital status can see others as souls and feel connected. We can feel connected as fellow humans having similar life experiences. We can observe the uniqueness of life, value love, and touch another person's essence. We can connect, grow, and expand. I like to think energy healing and listening to a person's needs are ways to touch the innermost part of the soul. Now this wonderful patient had expressed this thought so joyfully and powerfully.

I mentioned to this patient that a medium had only recently told me I was known as Sarah in another place about 2,000 years ago. Our soul energy is forever alive, having experiences that continue to refine our awareness of our human and divine capabilities, and our experiences are ongoing. One life could never be enough for us to evolve into higher conscious beings. The woman asked me to help her open her hand, which, because of the weakness of her muscles, was clenched tightly. I gently did so and held her hand for a while. We both seemed grateful to have crossed each other's path. I left the room with her hopeful words for continued peace and gentleness to prevail.

As I wandered out, I heard two men mentioning their brother and realized they were relatives of the man I had visited last week. He had not passed yet, and I wished to tell the father about his wonderful son Michael, who had played the guitar for me and was so attentive to his ailing uncle. The bond between the younger man and older man was beautiful. Michael, without hesitation, had offered to teach my little Samantha how to play the guitar. Such openness of heart and soul is becoming more prevalent in my meetings with strangers. I guess by having become more open and joyful to everyone I meet, the same energy is being brought to me.

I was so glad to meet the brother of the man to whom I had spoken last week. He told me that his dying brother was a beautiful man, giving to everyone, and he never had any regard for money but only for what it could do to ease another person's difficulty. He played a song he had written for his brother's funeral service with words that spoke of being up high in God's service and with loved ones beyond pain and ordinary life. They were words of exultation and freedom. I told him the messages in his words were the truths I had garnished in readings from Spirit and that the message was always dressed in garments of love and peace. We were encouraged to learn more of those wonderful godly virtues and to incorporate them into our lives.

We are definitely evolving into people with higher consciousness and awareness of our human and spiritual energetic essence. Many souls in the days to come will try to help others live a more valued existence with this knowledge. Regardless of the negativity and greed of some people who have put this nation and, indeed, the world in a financially and socially unbalanced position, I still feel those who are striving for spiritual enlightenment will restore and overcome these less-evolved individuals.

Returning to my office after hospice, Brian told me a story of coincidence about his son Michael, and I was still remembering the Michael who cared for his uncle in hospice.

Brian said, "Well, I have a coincidence for you. My son was away at college and went into the post office to pick up a package. In front of him was another student. The man handed him three packages, and the boy said, 'I was expecting one.'"

"Here are three with the same name, Michael Katz," said the post-office employee.

"Well," Brian's son said, "I am also Michael Katz." And the boy in front said, "I am Michael Katz also."

I told Brian that this story of his son reminded me of a time when I flew on a plane and was in my assigned seat. A woman came and said, "This is my seat." She had the same name as me, Sheryl Glick.

Brian said, "But what does it mean?"

I am so surprised when someone, especially those people I think understand, want answers to questions or happenings that are simply unanswerable and need only to be accepted for their uniqueness and the possibilities they provide for us to think and feel in a more open-hearted way. Perhaps when we ask to know more, we are merely hungry, curious, and anxious to know life on a deeper level.

I just said, "Well, I guess it might mean that we are supposed to meet that person to share an ordinary experience that could awaken us to a higher level of conscious knowing. Maybe we are not alone and there is a higher life force securing all our goings and comings. Or we might just enjoy the magical moment with humor and a smile. In order to do this, we need to put aside our analytical mind, which is hard for most of us, and find the mystery of life within our heart.

CHAPTER 14
Challenges Move Us Forward

We must live through the dreary winter,
if we would value the spring
And the woods must be cold and silent,
Before the robins sing.

The flowers must be buried in darkness,
Before they can bud and bloom.
And the sweetest, warmest, sunshine,
Comes after the storm and gloom.
Agnes L. Pratt

There are possibilities in this world and beyond when you step out of your limitations, fears, and doubts and show more regard for different states of mind and belief systems. Some people, however, are not able to let go of their deeply embedded belief systems and shift to a radically different approach to navigating life. The change could be too drastic and damage the way they perceive themselves and how they function.

My husband has made no pretense to me about his thoughts of an afterlife. He firmly announces there are no mediums, and I believe without holding onto his deeply embedded beliefs, the physical world would be difficult for him. The funny part is that David has sent me clients with serious, life-threatening, emotionally devastating issues.

He has seen the reactions of people he has sent and the results, yet he is grappling with the idea that spiritual healing is at work in helping these people. Perhaps he wants to give me these great challenges sub-consciously, intuitively knowing I will provide some assistance. As an attorney, his logical mind needs visual and tangible immediate results, and energy healing and spiritual development are often slow, challenging processes fostering change not in the materialistic way, but in the way of soul life.

> *Change comes so hard for all of us, yet we all must march*
> *and dance courageously to the song of our own heart*
> *and higher selves, especially as our soul matures.*

We must be quiet and listen to the thoughts of the mind and reach deep inside for higher knowing? Will you allow it?

❖

This Saturday, a former client brought her friend Amy for a session. Amy had read my book and immediately told me of all the synchronicity she had with me. She was married to an attorney in Albany. They divorced, and it was years later and she was now seeing a boyfriend with the same name as her ex-husband. Their twin daughters were born on September 16th, which is my birthday. One of them is studying to be a rabbi. This reference reminds me that my mother had said to me when I was a child that perhaps one day, I would be a rebbetzin, or rabbi's wife.

After the session a day later, she e-mailed me and validated all the messages I had given her. She thanked me for an amazing experience. Then she asked, "What does all this mean?"

This reminded me that recently Brian asked me that very same question. I knew on her soul level, she believed everything was happening as it should and that a higher realm of loving energy was guiding her. On another level, her mind, she still had doubts and wished to know what to do with these amazing coincidences. Perhaps there is nothing to do but be in the presence of awareness and joy for the gift of having a unique experience.

A few days later, when I was again at hospice, it seemed to me that wonderful experiences are tied and woven together in order to achieve a new level of serving others effortlessly, leaving lightness of love and being in their wake. As I walked into the sunroom, I saw a young girl lying on the rattan love seat. She seemed quiet and tired. I decided to see if there was anything, I could get for her. She very much reminded me of my new daughter-in-law, Lea: small and delicate, yet strong in a quiet way.

Julie is from San Francisco and told me she is a twin and her other sister was in with their father. I mentioned the story of my client Amy and her twin daughters, who were born on September 16th, my birthday, and the aunt who had just joined us said that was her anniversary date. We continue to share stories of similarities. The uncle's name was Gregory or Gregg. We all felt so grateful to have met, and we went in to see their father and send him our most loving intentions for a safe journey home.

❖

Where does life begin and end? Perhaps the questions should be, "What is life? What is death?" The Western world has still to expand its thinking on the end of life. Instead of thinking of the soul passing into nothingness, if we saw it as a remarkable passage through time and space, a reunion with loved ones, we could be joyful instead of sad.

We need to further investigate and begin to understand the energetic laws of the Universe. As energy can never be destroyed, only transformed, the energetic process of the mind and heart must exist beyond the physical body. I try to think back to the time when this belief was as foreign to me as the belief that life existed on the moon. I can hardly remember that time any longer, for there have been so many wonderful connections between people and Spirit since then.

It is painful for me to see people who suffer, because often, they have no understanding of the power or influence of the invisible, divine world over our human environment and therefore are not able to take comfort in the thought that even in the most difficult of times, we are being guided and loved.

Many people have had dreams of their deceased relatives and friends. Some people have felt or seen departed loved ones. For those who have experienced such events, some will never again doubt the accuracy of their own experiences. Others may call it hallucination or the power of suggestion or imagination. Those who experience these intimate spiritual encounters and recognize them usually consider the gift a real miracle.

Only the other day while at hospice, Sabrina, one of the aides, wanted to tell me a funny story of how she had an interactive dream with her dad, who had died ten years ago. In the dream, Sabrina's father told her to buy two doves to keep her mother company. Sabrina did, and the doves later had two babies. Only one survived. Now, she had three doves, and they brought her mother so much pleasure.

"Wow," I said, "Maybe your dad met up with my mom in Spirit and knew that somehow down the road, we would need to have this conversation. The message my mom promised to send me, if she arrived safely in the next dimension, was three doves."

Spirits are so smart and their love so strong that they can make a path to those who are special to them here on earth. Though we share only a moment with another soul, that moment could be one of eternal love.

CHAPTER 15
Look to The Rainbow for Love

Whenever you are sincerely pleased, you are nourished.
Ralph Waldo Emerson

I wish to remember and share with others a day of special events with powerful messages for me. This special day began as I walked into my treatment room followed by a little boy named Liam. Liam was about four years old. "This is a doctor's office," he said.

I told him, "This is my room, where people can relax, breathe deeply, and begin to know themselves better."

He repeated, "This is a doctor's room, and my mother needs to come here." Liam's mother, Elizabeth, was sitting right outside. Elizabeth had studied Reiki in the past and was a physical therapist. Elizabeth asked Liam if he would like to come to me for a session and she would come also. Liam said "yes," and in a session, we might find out more about his special talents and needs. Elizabeth told me she would call and arrange the appointments. The expression "From the mouths of babes comes great truth" has credence.

Sylivia's Passing

My husband's mother, Sylvia, was diagnosed with kidney failure. She was 93, and the last time I saw her, months ago, her last words to me were, "I want to live." I think she knew her time was winding down, but also knew how precious life was and how much she loved life. When David and his brother opted to begin kidney dialysis, I was not happy. As a hospice volunteer for the last six years, I believed with all my heart that our essence, or soul, survives physical death and energetic bonds of love exist eternally. I accept this circle of life.

The time before crossing over should be a time of reflection. We should help people be comfortable with the process of dying as we help the family accept the change. Caring professionals seem essential to this end, and I believe that palliative care, no extraordinary means being used to prolong life, should be followed in a hospice facility that deals with end-of-life issues.

But the choice was not mine to make in Sylvia's situation. Many loved ones will do anything to keep their family member with them, and the doctors offer treatments to that end even when the outcome is already known. Three weeks passed with this treatment plan, and then Sylvia passed quietly in her sleep. I believe that was a blessing.

At the time of Sylvia's funeral, my son, Gregg, and his wife, Lea, were on their honeymoon in Italy. My daughter, Stacey, and her husband, Jeremy, announced they were going to have identical twins. Stacey was ten weeks pregnant.

I had weddings and bat mitzvahs over the summer and felt there would soon be some funerals along the trail. We come and go, enjoy and endure, as the wheels of life and love spin and we are endlessly given opportunities to see the circle of life and death.

I am so proud and grateful for the wonderful
family members and friends at my side.

❖

After Sylvia's funeral service, Francine, a cousin who loved Sylvia like a mother, called and told me that her mother, Mary, almost 102 years old and in hospice care, had gotten out of bed during the middle of the night. She was found in the hallway of the nursing facility, crying. She kept saying over and over again, "She is dead," at about the time that Sylvia had passed. No one in the nursing facility knew what to make of it.

Perhaps a soul whispers as they leave the earth plane
to someone who needs a whisper of love.

❖

A few nights ago, I was invited to present an introduction to Reiki at a client's restaurant. The place was noisy, and I wasn't sure if I would be able to receive messages to share. Of course, I should not have doubted that those in Spirit who wished to connect would, even in an environment that was noisier than my office. The first message delivered was from a sister in Spirit who had died long ago from leukemia. Her sibling, present this night, sorely missed her.

These very tears of love and gratitude this sister shared are the response when one realizes the truth of continuous eternal life and of beyond, which is a realization like no other. This connectedness between different dimensions during energy sessions is more than comforting. If we come to know that this life is preparation for life on the next level, we enthusiastically pursue spiritual wisdom and undertakings to advance our growth and enter future worlds.

Resolving wounded feelings from past relationships is also part of this spiritual process, which, when completed, allows for a greater state of peace. Peace moves us to truth and beauty beyond the physical and joy beyond any living expression of happiness. It is the ultimate moment of connection to the God force.

Mother Teresa once said, "To pray is to believe, to believe is to love, and to love is to serve." A prayer is only a moment of gratitude and self-aware-ness of soul energy and positive thoughtful intention. Everything mirac-ulous flows from the simplicity of that element and mode of thought in conjunction with Spirit.

At the office, my client Trisha, whom I haven't seen in some time, approached me with a smile, and I was reminded of how she had first come to me four years ago for a reading and Reiki energy session. Trisha was a teacher, married, happy, and wanted a child. After several readings and healing sessions, it became apparent to me that one day she would have a son. I sensed little blue booties touching down ever so lightly on the ground. It was not long after that vision that Trisha became pregnant. Soon into that pregnancy, I received a phone call from a breathless, fright-ened Trisha telling me that her husband, Matt, had experienced a medical emergency and was in the hospital with a collapsed lung. Trisha asked me to accompany her to the hospital, where I conducted an energy session, and Matt allowed himself to relax and was very thankful for my presence even though he had severe pain that caused sweat to appear on his brow and chin. At this moment, Trisha was so overwhelmed by her husband's situation that she could barely think of the baby and her own health.

A few days passed, and Matt came home from the hospital, Trisha called and asked me if I could come to their house and give Matt another session. When I arrived at the door and saw Trisha's face distressed and pale, I asked in a concerned voice, "Is everything all right?"

Trisha responded that she had just come from an appointment with her doctor and was in shock, as was the doctor, who told her the baby's heartbeat was gone and a procedure to eliminate the fetus was required. Realizing how sad Trisha was, Matt asked me to work with Trisha first. As Trisha lay on the bed and the soothing music played, some thoughts floated through my mind and I said, "This soul was not ready to come at this time, but you'll be pregnant again very shortly. Everything is just as it should be, and there's nothing anyone did wrong to create this set of circumstances. You and Matt have time to bond more closely together in your love and realize that our destinies are not fully in our hands. It is through our thoughts and actions that precious moments of awareness from Spirit surrounds us during these challenging times. A few months later Trisha was pregnant, and in the right time her daughter, Amy, was born.

Here was Trisha, years later, and as she turned the stroller around, she said, "This is my son, Zach." A smile appeared on my face as I remembered what I had told her four years ago about a little boy. Sometimes an intuitive might sense something, but it doesn't always happen exactly in the time frame that the mind perceives it.

Whose plan is at work in our lives? Much of it seems to be divine intention coupled with our own wishes and needs for our souls to experience the most out of our physical lives.

❖

As I drove to hospice, the skies darkened, and I was sure that before too long, there would be snowflakes covering my windshield. As I drove, I wondered why I had to learn how to transport a patient in a wheelchair. Each year I took continuous hospice training, and I had never had to take a patient in a wheelchair. I told myself I would never have to use that skill.

I arrived at hospice. Sabrina, a very pleasant, gifted aid, suggested I go into a certain room. I appreciate when the staff directs me to those they feel will best be served by a visit. There was a young man, his son, his father, and his brother. The patient was a man about 49 years old, and his son was 14. They were from Florida but were here in New York because their family lived here. They needed help now that he was fighting a very invasive disease. We all talked. The father of the patient let me know his second wife was in a hospital in Manhattan, also being treated for a serious illness. His first wife had died years before. I sensed this man had been able to be a caretaker for others because of his strong faith. He was a protective, enduring person. Not only do the ill suffer, but those who care for them are also challenged to avoid suffering and remain healthy, uplifted, and hopeful.

Suddenly we noticed snowflakes falling, and within a few minutes, enough accumulated to make the open plains beyond the building glisten and shine with freshness. The patient wanted to go outside to smoke, and he told his son to get a nurse to help them. I said that that would not be necessary as I was trained to take him. He was so thrilled not to have to wait. I told the patient "This is the first time I've done this, so if we cooperate, we can show the staff how expert we are at this maneuver."

I was acutely aware that only an hour ago, I had said to myself I would never have to do this. Was the Universe saying, "Never say never," or did I intuitively pick up that I would have to help this man by using a wheelchair? It might be that the Universe gives us what we most want, or what we do not want, as it doesn't analyze it but just delivers it. Make sure of where your concentration and thoughts are, as they are crucial in manifesting your reality.

As we joyfully left the room and made our way to the outside sun porch, I was grateful for my training and for being able to be of service in this small way. Father and son went outside, and I watched through the large window, as I had no coat. They threw snowballs at each other, and both turned with wondrous smiles towards me.

I smiled back and realized that often the most gratifying and special moments we share with each other cannot be planned. They unfold according to a most divine plan. This is a compassionate and universal form of love that each of us seeks to experience. When it truly happens, often we don't recognize it for the precious gift that it is. It was exciting to be able to participate in this awakened moment of my heart and the hearts of these two men.

While the father smoked, the boy came in, and I had the chance to tell him what a loving, good son he was and how lucky they were to have each other. I knew the boy was saddened and frightened by his dad's illness. I told him to remember the fun with snow in days to come and his love for his dad. As I wheeled the father back to his room, I told him it was a pleasure to see him and his son share a good time together. Focusing on the most beautiful of his thoughts and memories would help him on his journey towards the future...one filled with love and the beauty of our spirits.

I am amazed at how effortlessly our loved ones in Spirit try to maneuver us in ways so we may find help for accepting loss and death. I would like to believe they hope to teach us that there is only transcendence, a different experience for us beyond this life that we cling to so fearfully.

Throughout my hospice work, while meeting many people, I saw that people who held on at the end of life often had experienced many challenging times during their life and they were accustomed to adversity and struggle. That appeared to be why dying seemed difficult for them, as they so courageously fought to survive. Those who have had a different life experience and have been blessed with a good family, quality education, good health, and wonderful opportunities and experiences to explore the vast potential of life knowing something more lies ahead, do not fight at the end of life, in the same way as the others who have struggled all their lives, and as a result, have an easier transition. It is often hard for me to know what to do and say to help people struggling at the end of life. Often, just listening to music or poems of friendship or watching television is calming. I just try to smile and show my love for life as it unfolds in its own way, accepting it all without reservation. Most people seem comfortable with that expression.

CHAPTER 16
Gentle Souls Fully Awakened

The millions are awake enough for physical labor, but only one in a million is awake enough for effective intellectual exertion, only one in a hundred million to a poetic or divine life. To be awake is to be alive.
Henry David Thoreau, *Walden*

This day was like a spring interlude in a winter season that was cold, blustery, snowy, and full of incessant colds and illness. Today was a glimpse into the spring that lay ahead and a reminder that even a moment of sunshine and warmth delights our hearts and souls.

I was at a meeting for the Academy of European Art and Culture. Annalisa and Fayina had reviewed my one-year involvement with this Fourth Way School, which is populated by creative, soulful people who seek a higher connection and understanding of life, energy, and their own physical being. By understanding how we respond from either a soul perspective or a physical perspective, we hope to foster a higher connection to the Divine, a better quality of interactions with others, and a more forgiving way of proactively dealing with everyone. Then everything is possible.

I have not been able to completely devote myself to the work of this school, as I am still involved in many other pursuits leading ultimately to the same ends. Yet I have benefitted greatly from the sharing of works of art and literature and from the beauty of soul and intelligence that the people in the group have. After our talk, the other members come into the room. We began the discussion of a chapter from a book called *The Theory of Conscious Harmony*.

I noticed Carolina as she sat across from me. Every once in a while, I discovered that she jotted a note in her little journal. At some point, she looked at me intensely, and as I focused on her loving, peaceful face, there was an actual shift of energy. I saw her as a double image. Perhaps this was the soul essence stepping away from the body to be an observer of the proceedings. I had never seen anything like this. I continued to watch the energy field above her enlarge, and I saw a profile of a woman with a covered head and below her, a large man in a brown robe. His head was also covered. As a medium, while in meditation, I have observed spiritual energy forms, retrieved information, and sensed images of other souls, but I have never seen it this way with my eyes fully open. I am aware that some mediums express that they see someone above them and someone below, representing two different generations as a parent and child perhaps.

I am humbled by the feeling of these gentle souls who allow me to see them, if only for a moment. I feel them to be religious figures of antiquity. After the meeting, Carolina sat by me, and I asked, "Do you know what I saw?" She did not. When I described the images, Carolina said, "I prayed for you to see Jesus and Mary." Tears came to my eyes. Whatever had I done in this life to deserve the opportunity for a moment like this? I was so moved and grateful for this moment of divine grace and love.

Several weeks later, my longtime student Barbara, also now a Reiki master, came to me for a session. She had often said that seeing Spirit might be hard or frightening for her. I related my story of having seen Spirit with my eyes open and that it was an awesome and wonderful experience. I had no fear, only astonishment. As we began her reading, the first message was, "Like a feeling that the soul and essence stand above and detached from the physical pain or fear of the body. It feels like an uplifting and connection to the beauty of spirit: powerful and like being out and in the body at the same time."

"Barbara," I said in surprise. "I haven't looked at this reading since weeks ago. It seems to describe what we were just talking about." Perhaps as our abilities expand and change, we are able to see the spiritual energy of loved ones, relatives, or guides in this way. It is just another way to gather information from the different realms of energy and life forces, and we can make deeper, more visual connections.

❖

Years have passed, and I now have four granddaughters. The twins, Chelsea and Talia, are an amazing way for me and others to experience the energy of soul life, for while they look alike in so many ways, they are unique.

One summer day, my four-year-old granddaughter Chelsea saw me lay down on the sofa. It was a hectic, hot day, and I thought I would take a 15-minute rest. Chelsea covered me with blankets from head to toe and then placed a tissue over my forehead. She put her hand over the tissue, and I instantly felt so relaxed and rested. No one had shown her how to do this. Healers, it seems are born, not made. It seems the sensitivity to observe and help others is a human instinct that can be fostered by love. Years later on a Facebook posting, I saw a doctor show how to help infants fall asleep instantly by placing a tissue over their foreheads.

CHAPTER 17
Lucky Girl, Lucky Life

*This was the simple happiness of complete harmony
with her surroundings, the happiness that asks for
nothing, that just accepts, just breathes, just is.*
Countess Van Arnim (English writer, 1866 - 1941)

When I returned from my trip where I had met many women named Susan, I decided to check the derivation of the name Susan in a book of names that I owned. I found that Susan was from the Hebrew derivation meaning lily or purity, and a lily is also a white flower. I like to think real love is pure, sincere, and undeniable.

I have searched actively to sense and recognize that beautiful capacity of love that people might possess but find it is all too rare. Too many people are disconnected from their divine soul essence, and love cannot flourish without this connection to the Universal Source of life. Perhaps I wish to perfect this quality within myself in order to see it more clearly in others.

The pure heart, mind, and soul, like those I imagine the gatekeepers of heaven to possess and the songs of the Universe they sing, bring us closer to remembering we are love when we allow ourselves to love life in all of its many aspects. Recently, a medium at a workshop told me to listen to the vibration and words of Frank Sinatra's version of *Moonlight Serenade*: "I stand by your gate in the moonlight and bring you a moonlight serenade of love."

Moonlight Serenade reminded me to be fully in appreciation for my own human and soul existence. Self-love is necessary first in the chain of loving all.

On Wednesday night, April 16th, the first day of Passover, I visited several patients at the Glen Cove nursing facility, where I volunteered for hospice work.

The first woman I visited today was from Italy and talked with fondness about her family and her life. She was extremely energized and happy to see me, and her eyes lit up like two bright suns reflecting down on me. I told her my grandpa used to call me *Sherala* with his lovely Russian accent, exactly the same way she did with her lovely Italian accent. She smiled, and I told her I enjoyed our visit and would see her after Easter with some Easter treats. Then I visited another new patient, who was hooked up to an oxygen machine. She was alert and talkative even though her breathing was labored, and her cough sounded like gurgling or fluid in her lungs. She wanted so much to go to the birthday party in the dining hall, but the nurse said she couldn't because of the hookup. I went to the dining hall and brought back two pieces of cake.

On the way back, I ran into Sonya who was a patient I often noticed sitting alone in the hallway. I stopped to acknowledge her, and she asked for a piece of cake. After bringing her cake from the dining hall, I stayed with her while she ate it. Sonya dug in with her fingers, and it was quite a gooey and messy cake. I went to get paper towels, and she told me she liked to eat like this now. I remembered when my mom did that, I made a judgmental statement about her way of eating and reprimanded her, telling her to use a fork. It seems older people, or people with physical illness, sometimes lose their social graces, as it becomes harder for them to do the simple acts of living. They spend so much time alone. Maybe it hardly seems necessary to put on a civilized show. I was sorry I was not as understanding and compassionate with my own mom as I now was to Sonya. I mentioned to Sonya that I had a hospice client in another location and her name was Sonya also. She had told me that many Sonyas and Sophies liked to be called Sue, the more modern interpretation.

Following my conversation with Sonya, I went in to visit another patient whose aide was by her side. The aide told me that she came from a very large family but had only one daughter. "My one daughter is Susan."

On the way out, I saw Sonya was in the same place I had last seen her. When she saw me, she said, "Wherever you're going, I'm going." We went to the lunchroom, and I told Sonya to go enjoy the others, as I had another appointment to see someone who was very sick. She said, "I'm very sick." All she wanted was to have someone stay with her.

That night at a group meeting, I met someone new and was talking about all the recent connections to the name Susan. This man said, "My wife is Susan." I told him that I had looked into the derivation and origin of the name to see what energy and qualities were associated with the name. "Well," he said, "My wife, Susan, is very home-oriented and tells it like it is. She doesn't beat around the bush and can be somewhat blunt, but no matter how difficult things are, she tries to keep it together."

I had been told some time ago at a meeting of The International Spiritual Federation by a Swedish medium, an artist, Sonya, that I would be a medium. Another reference to the Susan stories I had been investigating. I had difficulty accepting the prediction that I would become a medium, although Sonya drew a picture that looked so much like my mother, whom she had never met, depicting her beautiful brown eyes and dark eyebrows. Knowing my mother could be seen by this medium, I simply thought I just had to get my book published so people could be as amazed as I was that death was not the final curtain. This message from Sonya (Susan) helped me become aware that my life contract and purpose were to develop this gift of communicating with spirits.

People in my development group have given me many messages. The relatives relaying information to them are as they were in life, most articulate and persistent in getting it all to me. A good communicator in life is always a good one from beyond. One of the men in the group asked me if someone had passed recently, and I said no. He told me someone would pass, and it would be a male. They were waiting for him, and there was nothing that could be done. I thought it might be my uncle who was ill. Several weeks later, I learned that his son Alan had passed.

Another participant mentioned large wings and added that out of the wings flew several doves, and I knew that this message was from my mom, who had promised to get that very message of the doves to me from the other side. Still another man told me he sensed the movie *Gone with the Wind*. References to the themes in that movie seem to be appropriate to my own life, perhaps reminiscent of changes in my life, from the frivolous to the more worthwhile values I now possess, such as my growing love for others and the finding of an unbridled and expansive love for life.

Amazing Boardwalk Encounters

I was walking on the boardwalk on Sunday morning. It was the first beautiful, warm, breezy, sunny day, and I was happy to know that the long, most difficult winter New Yorkers had faced in many years was finally over. At the end of my walk, I sat down on one of the memorial benches. Many new memorial benches had been added to the boardwalk in these last few years since the attack on Twin Towers. As I watched the ocean and slowly grounded myself in meditation to the earth, I let the energy flow through me, practiced deep breathing, and began a silent meditation. My intention on this day was to ask if I was wisely using the many God-given talents that I had become cognizant of. On this particular day, I observed in my inner vision in meditation that a group of seven souls in shadow surrounded me, and it was a comforting feeling. I asked for a sign during or after the meditation to help guide me. I had a wonderful quiet time and then felt quite energized.

As I walked over to a bench where a small bunch of flowers had been placed, I read the dedication that simply said, "You are the love of my life." There was no name on this bench, so I looked at the bench next to it, and it was dedicated to Cecile. Everyone called my mom Ceil, but I would not be surprised if on her birth certificate it was Cecil or Cecilia, as those were names that were used at the time my mom was born. I walked a little farther and stopped at another bench, and the words were, "Beneath my Wings," which was the song from the movie *Beaches*. When I had a reading, years ago, I was told by my mom in Spirit to rent that movie, as it related to the end of her life and love she had for me. The movie is one of love and dedication between two women who stayed close to each other throughout whatever they perceived as failures of their relationship.

In actuality, there is no failure, only experiences to show us a greater love in all relationships.

I walked a little farther, and the next bench had beautiful fresh flowers attached to it also. Loved ones remembered whether in body or soul. It read, "One moment in time," and had my father's birth date. I believed those words answered my meditation question. You can only take life one moment at a time and one step at a time. No one could go faster or do more than we were already trying to do. As I stood looking at the bench, two women walked up to me. We began to talk, and I told them that I was observing the message on the bench. One of the women then said to me, "Are you a psychic?" I was surprised by this observation and said, "Why, do I look like a psychic, and what does a psychic look like?" I remarked that I was writing a book that was about spiritual concepts and psychic development.

One of the women said that she had twins, and they had brought her much joy, even though she hadn't expected twins. In retrospect, years after this meeting, my daughter Stacey had twin girls, Chelsea and Talia, who have brought so much joy and sensitivity to our family and were truly quite a miracle. We all thoroughly enjoy their gentle loving natures, and I am aware from my guides that many of the children being born during these changing and challenging times will have and hold a tremendous sense of goodness from Spirit and will help their elders become more aligned to their own innocence.

The women left, and I continued to walk over to a bench with two balloons attached. I stopped and read the three lines, "You touched each differently in different ways, did your best every day, with kind, loving, special ways." Next to it were three hearts. It was dedicated to Jerry, and I smiled, remembering my tiny plastic doll Jerry, the doll of my childhood. The message of this bench was clear to me. I was doing well.

Days later, it was warm and pleasant, so I drove to the boardwalk, as was my usual way, to be as close to nature. As I pulled into a parking space very close to the water, a car passed me, and a man in his late seventies who looked just like my uncle Hy was driving the vehicle. I remembered that I had intended to call my Aunt Lily and Uncle Hy during the last two weeks but had gotten busy and forgotten. My uncle was my mother's last living sibling. He was now 85 years old. Before my mother, Ceil, passed, she told Hy that he would make it to 92. I always thought that was her way of making him feel better about her impending passing and showed her wish to protect him from his fear of death. I walked for a short time under the sun and beauty of the moment, and when I was ready to leave, I walked towards the car. Another man passed me, and he looked even more like my uncle than the last man I had seen. I actually couldn't take my eyes off him, and when he said hello, I muttered hello in a strange way and turned to look at him again, this time seeing him from behind. I was amazed. Even from this view he looked just like my uncle. I approached the exit from the boardwalk, and another man who looked like my uncle walked up the ramp. In rapid succession, three men who looked like Hy, all in the same location and all who passed by me. This was no coincidence. Driving home, I was quite intent on calling my aunt and uncle immediately before leaving for work. My uncle was not home, but I had a nice talk with my Aunt Lily. She seemed to be able to accept some of these synchronicities more so than most of the other members of our conventional middle-class, Jewish-American family, maybe due to her Greek background. When I told her of the men who looked like Uncle Hy, she wasn't surprised. Aunt Lily said Uncle Hy looked very much like her dad. She also said that two weeks before her father died, she had a dream that he had died and didn't tell her mother. She knew there was no way to stop it. It seemed I was actually meant to hear this story about Aunt Lily's father, and perhaps that is why I saw all these men resembling my uncle. Perhaps it was Aunt Lily's father imprinting his energy on the men who walked by me because he wanted me to get a message to his daughter that he was still nearby.

A year later, at an event hosted by John Edward, a psychic medium, he discussed with great enthusiasm this process I had observed with my uncle, and I now knew Spirit could physically share their soul energy and imprint it onto another person. John called it "Spirit Overlay." He described it as souls projecting their personality and likeness onto a living person. I was happy to have validation for what I experienced, and now it had a very descriptive name.

CHAPTER 18
Breaking Free and Going into the Light

What's meant to be will always find a way.
Trisha Yearwood

So many miracles, small and large, have been happening this past week.

Just the other day, I went to see a foot reflexologist who was also a medium. She told me that I was the light and the messenger of truth for my entire family. My spiritual progress and breaking out of my restrictive, limiting childhood had put me on the right track. Those in Spirit were very proud of me. She told me my father said that the volunteer work I was doing with hospice was also a connection to my healing work and he felt I actually should be paid for it. My father also responded that my older sister had trouble understanding concepts of an afterlife, as she was too fearful, as were so many other people. However, many people I was talking to were listening. My dad also said he spent much time in my sister's house and the little dog didn't like him and barked whenever he was around. The medium also mentioned that my daughter, Stacey, had experienced an ectopic pregnancy that had just ended, and it was because that particular soul was not ready. The soul had gotten cold feet at the last minute. There would be another pregnancy, and my daughter should not be afraid. My dad said to get a room ready for the new baby. Our loved ones on the other side are really quite interested and actively participate in our progress. My dad wanted it to be known that many of the quiet thoughts that came to me when I walked on the boardwalk were his encouraging words.

My dad went on to mention that Brian Katz at the office was much inspired by my work. Many people at the office have supported, encouraged, and participated in my events, making shifts and improvements to their own life journey. Brian's encouragement and light had unwittingly initially opened the door to Spirit and all the new projects and investigations that I was involved in, as Brian was the one who suggested I read *The Celestine Prophecy*, which piqued my imagination and ultimately guided me to the study of quantum psychics and metaphysical concepts, leading me to become a Reiki Master Teacher and medium.

There was so much love being sent from beyond and from those who watched over me, sharing much gratitude and encouragement for the days ahead.

I was learning so much from my hospice patients and my clients who came to me at my office. Margaret arrived for her scheduled session and had let me know at her last appointment the reason she was coming for Reiki sessions. It was her desire to become pregnant and have a large family, but it wasn't happening as quickly as she had hoped. On this visit today, she looked especially healthy and happy. She told me that when she went to see her team of five doctors a few days ago after her last Reiki session, she had been given a sonogram. Her left ovary, which had been cystic, was now clear.

During the last session, Margaret had felt an unusual sensation like a breaking up or crumpling in that area. At the same time, I had felt something being dispersed or exiting. We didn't know what that meant at the time. We then continued her regular Reiki sessions, a gentle, noninvasive approach for anyone anywhere and in any circumstance.

There are usually a pleasant sensation and energy exchange for the practitioner and for the client during a session. Some people described it as expanded awareness, and others described it as tension melting away. Still others said it is balancing the mind, body, and soul. For this particular session with Margaret, I became aware of beautiful colors flowing through me and around the young woman. During the session, I sensed a large, green field with hills and farmhouses in the background. Margaret told me that she had been married in such a beautiful spot, and she was thinking that someday she would show her future children this place. I also sensed a four-leaf clover and a green angel or fairy rising into the sky. The young woman said she and her grandmother shared the same name and birth date and loved the St. Patrick's Day Parade. I was pleased with the messages and the enthusiasm and dedication Margaret had for the Reiki experience. I looked forward to pictures of her children, as I knew it was only a matter of time before she would be pregnant.

Sometime later down the road, I was scheduled for an Arch Energy Training course sponsored by the Life Learning Center in Manhattan. A flyer advertising energy healing had come to my office while I was on vacation. The staff thought it was for me, as it was addressed to simply "Energy Healer." I immediately knew I must go to the course, for in the brochure, the words "rainbow healing" caught my attention. Reiki healers work with the seven main chakras or energy points of the body which exemplify the seven colors of the rainbow.

The course teacher, Laurie Grant, explained how over the course of 15 years, she had taught the Usui Reiki healing system in Arizona. After developing a serious knee problem from a car accident, she went to Hawaii on crutches even though her doctor had discouraged this trip. While at the large healing stones opposite her hotel, she had a mystical experience and her knee was healed. In gratitude for the miracle, she promised to follow the messages given to her from the ancient Hawaiian kahunas, or healers. She was asked by Spirit to remain in Hawaii and continue to work with their help. In my intuitive opinion, the kahunas are similar in their lifestyle and their use of healing techniques to the Native American shamans or the Japanese Reiki energy healers.

On the second day of this Arch Energy training, I was standing on the platform waiting for my train in order to get to the second day of the course in the city. It was brutally cold, and I was tired after traveling early in the morning into the city two days in a row for this course. A young woman with curly, sun-streaked brown hair who resembled my cousin Susan stood next to me. I remarked to her that she looked so much like my cousin, and I have met a continuous flow of women named Susan recently with varied name derivations such as Sonya or Sophie. Coincidentally, she said to me that her name was actually Suzanne.

I felt and knew it wasn't a coincidence that we met and remarked that since life was no coincidence, we might have something to say or share with each other. The other day I saw a local church sign with these words: "Coincidences are God's way of being anonymous." Suzanne said she was the librarian at the local high school and I should contact her friend, who was the director of special programs at another local library I had recently applied to, The Long Beach Library, in order to arrange a workshop and demonstration of Reiki. I went on to explain that my book

Life Is No Coincidence was about discovering there really is an afterlife. I had observed since working with different forms of energy healing that many people were able to gather information from the energy of loved ones in another dimension. Without taking a breath, Suzanne told me her mom had died two years before from cancer on July 14th. The seventh was the day my mom died, and the 14th was the day my dad died. I then found out that Suzanne was recently married, and I asked if her mom had known her husband. She said no, but I insisted that her mother did know him and was present at the wedding. My intuitive gut feeling and also the fact that I felt my mother and father present at my daughter Stacey's wedding were the reasons I was so adamant. I believe loved ones are still connected to us and especially revel in the joy we experience in good times. And in the sad moments, they are there as well. I know many loved ones are around us almost all of the time, but especially for big gatherings. You might say we are never alone.

With a few tears in her eyes, Suzanne told me that not long ago, when she and her husband were sitting together in the living room, a jar fell off the table, and it was not even near the edge. She moved it to another spot even farther away from the edge to avoid a repeat. Days later, when she and her husband were together, it happened again. I suggested that perhaps her mother was showing her that she was nearby. Suzanne agreed. Suzanne was Jewish, and her education, like mine, did not include a focus on or knowingness of an afterlife. Our sensitive and inquisitive natures and our life experiences were providing knowledge of this in an experiential way.

Every good and bad experience seen correctly, is part of our life plan, selected by our soul in conjunction with other teachers in Spirit that have helped us prepare for this life. We are living out the story that we wrote before we were born.

❖

As I arrived at my nail salon, I had no idea that I was in for an amazing encounter and a story connecting many of the elements of coincidences in the previous stories in this book. I began to talk to a woman named Virginia, mentioning that I was an energy healer. She told me that her husband had been in a wheelchair and she had witnessed three miraculous healings for him. He was told he would never walk again due to a degenerative disc disease. One year ago, Virginia and her husband went to a church far from home. They had planned to spend a peaceful afternoon at a place known to be restful, green, lush, and beautiful. While at the church, a priest asked her husband if he would like to have a spiritual healing. Her husband gratefully accepted the unexpected offer. It wasn't long after that he began to make progress in his physical therapy sessions. Previously there had been no progress.

Encouraged by her husband's progress, Virginia did a series of St. Teresa Novena prayers, which is supposed to be done five days in a row and before 11 AM. There is an accepted Catholic belief that on the fifth day if you see a rose, your wish for health will be granted. Virginia's husband read in a book about a bouquet of roses. It seemed roses were making their presence known. Likewise, Virginia noticed roses on her shower curtain that she had not noticed before. Her husband continued to improve, and the doctors at Mount Sinai were stumped for an answer to his continuing recovery. The final healing her husband received was at Boston College at the church where one of their three sons had been married.

One might call this story a contrived, fantastic
fantasy, but I call it a reality of Divine Love.

❖

At a recent reading with my spiritual group, my father-in-spirit, Myron, said he was collaborating with me on this book and was bringing people to me who had corresponding stories that fit like a glove. Well, that explanation was as good as any for the amazing way I kept meeting people who seemed intimately attached.

I received a call from Rosemarie. At first, Rosemarie was overwhelmed by the diagnosis of fourth-stage lung cancer and rejected seeing me. A few days later, she decided to call and asked me to come to her house for a healing session. Rosemarie's friend whom I had met at a healing retreat in the Bahamas had recommended me to her dear friend to help her deal with this serious illness. It seemed I was obviously guided to see her. I have little control over the people I am meant to interact with. That is fine with me, as I realize I would not be given any situation that I could not handle. I immediately set up a time to visit her.

The next day, I drove to Rosemarie's house which was quite some distance away. Rosemarie was merely 42 years old, with minor children. As Rosemarie talked, she let me know her father and aunt both had died from lung cancer. Rosemarie always had this fear that she would die young. I sensed that our fears might predispose us to what will happen, or maybe our all-knowing soul knows the time of our departure. Either way, we have our life plan and since thoughts are very powerful and words more powerful, I would encourage people to think only the most uplifting thoughts and use kind, wise, encouraging words. Practice saying, "Delete," whenever you have a thought that could ultimately make the Universe deliver a negative reality from a fear being expressed and then create a thought that suggests something grand. I, myself, wake up each morning and say, "I am grateful I am in a fit and healthy body, and let's go out into the world and meet some wonderful people."

My work with Rosemarie began by telling her about the events leading to the work I do now and my awareness that my being there with her was no coincidence. Spirit desired for her to become close to loved ones through an energy session so Rosemarie could feel safe again. I showed her several breathing techniques to help her relax, which is part of every healing session. We listened to a divine, healing music CD together. At the end of the session, she expressed to me that she felt peaceful and told me she would schedule an appointment at the hospital for further tests, which she had not wanted to do prior to the Reiki session. During this session, I did not see as much color as I usually do. When the life force is strong and we are following our prescribed life events, the chakras or energy points give off greater color into our aura. Conversely, a dimming of our energy field reflects a lower level of health or joy in our life. I noticed there was a tingling going through my throat, indicating either a physical or spiritual blockage making Rosemarie unable or unwilling to say or speak certain facts. I sensed in my inner vision a circle of souls around her, and one soul had a particularly bright light above him, indicating to me that he was especially close to her. I also saw a golden star and a golden flower opening up. These symbols implied to me a measuring of the progress of her spiritual development. I hoped the beautiful environment that waited for her in Spirit was as bright and open as these golden symbols suggested. Later that night, my teacher told me Rosemarie would pass from this illness and be received by loved ones, including her father, who was the man leading the circle of souls. I began to cry as I do each time, I read this passage for the inevitability of the physical process she had to face. I always want to give us all more time in this life, but each soul knows full well the course that they follow. Rosemarie sensed that her father was around her during the session, and that comforted her greatly.

I am sure we all have loved ones on the other side, standing in our corner, giving us signs and messages, and guiding us with their love and eternal knowledge. As on earth, we each have the opportunity to raise our consciousness to make changes to improve the quality of our thinking and actions. Furthermore, we continue to have opportunities to refine our being.

CHAPTER 19
Souls Writing Our Own Story

A bird doesn't sing because it has an answer,
it sings because it has a song.
Maya Angelou

I was happily at Johnny Rockets, a favorite hamburger place of mine. I love hamburgers even though I know meat can hinder spiritual development. Health practitioners or spiritual teachers sometimes recommend a vegetarian diet. Doreen Virtue mentioned in her first book that her impressions improved immensely with a change of diet. Certain habits such as what, where, and when one likes to have meals are hard to change.

A young woman with dark hair in a ponytail sat down next to me. She commented on my red leather pocketbook, which was next to me on the counter. I mentioned that I bought it only recently at the Venetian Hotel in Las Vegas. She responded that she had been at the new Bellagio Hotel and was amazed at seeing the entire ceiling of the lobby decorated with magnificent fresh flowers. The fragrant aroma stayed with her long after she left the area. I remembered being delighted to be in the lobby of that beautiful hotel, where beside the fresh flowers, there were giant glass butterflies and dragonflies—fully fanciful, almost magical, and unreal in size. The beauty of the colors and the boldness of their design made these insects seem ready to take flight. These larger-than-life and lifelike insects complemented the other area of the lobby, in which multicolored flowers, giant in size and made of hand-blown glass, graced the ceiling. We continued to talk, and she told me about her married brother in North Carolina whose wife was in a wheelchair. She knew everything happened for a reason yet hoped for some improvement to her sister-in-law's disability. I told her the story of Virginia; whose husband was unable to walk but after a miraculous series of three spiritual energy healings was very much able to walk.

I remarked that we all had a life plan. Moreover, if being disabled or having any illness or handicap served the highest interest of that individual's soul life, then healing sessions would not alter that plan, though there might be new thoughts gleaned from the healing sessions that could help them achieve a healthier attitude and acceptance of their challenge. Then I told her that thoughts, fears, and childhood restrictions often bring about a realized effect. One of the clients I met recently always thought she would get lung cancer, and she did. The girl gasped and told me she was afraid of the same thing, as her father's side was rampant with cancer and her mother's side had heart disease. I responded that we were born into a specific family to have certain physical qualities relationships and challenges that might aid our individual soul destiny and life plan for our personal development and growth, but that did not necessarily mean we would have the same life outcomes from events or diseases as other family members. We might change any consequence or outcome by our choices, intentions, and attitudes, and what seemed inevitable might be rewritten as we changed our emotional inner world to write a new life story. I encouraged this lady to discard any thoughts of illness and focus instead on a long, healthy, prosperous life.

❖

I encountered a young caregiver, Michelle, while at my last hospice visit. She was somewhat sad and tired but happy to see me. She asked me to give her an interpretation or reading of her life, as she had heard I was a medium. Michelle suddenly started to cry. I asked her why she was crying and touched her arm. She responded that her mother, Anna, had died a year ago on June 27th, my sister Rodelle's birthday, and she had not gotten any signs from her and missed her so much.

Here was this lovely woman, desperately needing to know her mother was safe and still near to her. Dare I be so bold and connect with Anna's spirit right here, away from the quiet of my office where I was accustomed to doing readings? It has been told to me that no medium can know which soul will choose to connect to them. All souls, living and dead, choose through their own free will if they will come through, but I have found that the souls most called upon by a person do visit. Perhaps if Michelle had not cried and appeared so tired and sad or if she wasn't such a genuinely good, caring person, I might not have taken the chance to step out of my comfort zone to get a message for her. I closed my eyes and simply asked for some signs to soothe Michelle's sadness. I emptied my mind and set my ego and personal self to the side so I could be a clear channel. Before long, I sensed an opening, a field with tall grass, soft breezes, and not many houses, remote and rural with mountains in the distance. I sensed a shadow, and this soul radiated so much love for her land, for her daughter, and for her family. There was a glaring golden light around her. I also sensed two souls standing next to her, but she was the main interest for me. I asked Michelle if her mother had lived in that place that I was describing, and she said, "Yes, it was just like that in the Dominican Republic." Then I saw a statue of Mary and asked if that was in her mother's house. Something made me say Maria instead of Mary. Michelle said her mother's daughter-in-law was Maria, whom she had a loving relationship with and had left everything, all her earthly possessions, to after her death.

I sensed Michelle looked just like her mom. She said, "Yes, as a matter of fact, I do." Then I saw a Christmas tree with nothing on top, and magically, a pink angel and star appeared. I told Michelle what I saw, and she said in the past, she did not put anything on top of the tree, but this year she wanted a pink angel or star or both for her tree. I asked Michelle if the messages had relieved some of her fear about the passing of her mother. She responded that she was thrilled and grateful to know some part of her mother still existed and could still make her feel loved, even from afar.

Weddings, Bridal Showers, and Love

My husband, David, and I arrived at the fine, elegant catering facility at Eisenhower Park in Nassau. The day was bright, sunny, and perfect for a wedding. This past spring, the weather had been exceedingly cold, as if the snowy winter had not been willing to end. A sunlit day like this was a break for the families of the marrying couples and for all the guests. It was a beautiful ceremony, observed among large, magnificent bouquets of rainbow-colored flowers, sunshine, and a waterfall in the extensive gardens beyond.

Following the wedding ceremony, the guests moved rapidly outdoors. Everything was beautifully displayed and elegantly presented. Going over to our table, I took my seat right by the orchestra. The music was loud. I quickly found that three of the four women at my table were named Susan and were friends of the groom's mother, who was also Susan. Now, my husband, who is not as sensitive to these happenings, would not see any value in this congregation of women with the same name. However, after months of "Susan" roaming in and out of my vision, I was acutely aware that something was up. I asked questions of the women to find a commonality among them, but there were none. I did notice that the women appeared to be ordinary gals living ordinary lives, but each seemed to be facing challenges of one kind or another. People exploring Kabbalah, an ancient study of universal energy factors, believe that names and numbers are codes directing us towards certain inevitabilities in our life plans. They could indeed set up certain tendencies that lead to certain outcomes. Regardless of our name, without a spiritual interpretation and acceptance of destiny and fate, we could not empathize with other people's challenges or our own.

The wedding was great, and I had a good Susan story. There was lively music and good food. I proceeded home to a second party, a surprise shower for my editor, Mary, in a neighbor's house. I was late. Mary was the guest of honor and had not arrived yet. I was handed a folding chair and placed it in the only spot available in a room that was packed with people. I asked the two ladies to my right and to my left their names. Both responded, "Susan." I had met *seven* Susan's that day. I do believe, by anyone's standards, even skeptics would recognize this was unusual and probably not a coincidence.

The next night, before the group meeting started, I asked Barbara, my teacher, why she thought I was meeting so many women named Susan. Barbara believed that my guides were helping me absorb an understanding of the Susan energy or the life force of that name so I might recognize how life was set in motion for a person based on a plan made long before they received their earth name. She hoped that I could accept my own life path so different from all the women named Susan I had met.

Maybe by giving up a part of our independence as we age, one takes great spiritual strides towards trust in the Unseen.

CHAPTER 20
Serving As Soul's Escort

Love is how you stay alive, even after you are gone.
Mitch Albom

Guided by a Higher Hand

My daughter, Stacey, called me at my office. I was thrilled for a phone call during work hours, as this was not the norm. She had a most unusual story to tell me. She said, "Mom, something strange happened today, and I just called home to tell you what happened, but told Dad instead. I was on the train going to the 14th Street station and was on the first car. There was a lot of noise, and a man by the window yelled that someone had been pushed onto the tracks. Later, I found out that he was a student of martial arts and had the presence of mind to get into the center track, where there was a small cut-out spot. He lay down flat, and the train went over him. He survived. The conductor came out of his compartment and was visibly shaken." Stacey was shaken also. It later turned out that the man was the brother of one of Stacey's clients. Perhaps, there was a reason that Stacey needed to witness this horrific event.

Her question to me was, "Why was I in the first car today?"

My answer was, "We are in the right spot at the right time to make an observation that will ultimately be part of our awakening to a greater understanding and appreciation of life. A higher hand guides us."

I awoke the other night and suddenly thought of Christopher Reeve's Superman character and Tobey Maguire's Spider-Man character. It seemed both superheroes were aware of the great love held for specific women in their lives. I was reminded of the similarity between real-life, fiction and art. I had seen several articles of late about comic-book material being made into movies. What seems real in either life or art form, in reality or fantasy, is our growing capacity to love and to face life challenges. I am again aware that all that happens to us in life is part of a life plan reaching beyond to those in Spirit as a form of eternal life and divine love intermingling.

> *As we continuously fade into life, or fade out of life into Spirit, we are still and always loving, light beings guided and loved by God and his helpers. As human fear and doubt fade, it appears all souls shine a little brighter in the cosmic eternities.*

❖

Unexpected Kindness

At my nail salon, I met a woman who was from Lebanon. She told me a lovely story of unexpected kindness from a stranger. Her son had gotten three tickets in a very short time. She didn't tell her husband, as he would have exploded, so on the appointed day, she and her son went to the small courthouse in a town she couldn't remember the name of on the South Shore. They arrived early, and while waiting, a man came over and started a conversation. She told him the problem, and he said he was a lawyer and knew everyone in the courthouse. "I will help you," he said, and all the paperwork was completed in an expedient way. Then the lawyer said to the boy, "Now take your mom to a show." He wanted the boy to appreciate his mom for all her dedication and concern.

As I told her about my sister Suelle having a similar divine intervention with the attorney who appeared in her time of need and helped her out, I was hoping she might see that often more is going on than can be logically explained. She responded to me by saying that she was not quite sure we were all born with a plan designed exclusively for our soul growth and that the people we've encountered were part of that plan. Also, she was not fully aware of the role that psychics or mediums played in our lives.

However, she said she had gone to a psychic a few years before, and he only worked with a small number of people. She had been in this country since 1976 and had not returned to Lebanon, her native country. She told this intuitive person that she had a trip planned to Beirut, and the psychic said he sensed her going with her husband on a trip, but not to Beirut. A few days later, there was a political uprising and bombing in Beirut, so she canceled her trip and instead went with her husband to Canada for a family wedding. Her husband had planned to go without her while she was in Beirut, but plans changed just as the psychic had predicted. This psychic was so conscientious and concerned about her safety that he called to check if all was well and at that time found that what he had predicted had already transpired.

It seems to me that psychics often see something that will happen days, weeks, months, or years down the line. I believe that is because it has already transpired in some reality, as it appears time and space act on three connecting, concentric planes—intertwined, not linear—and our soul energy can be in different places and eras at once. So why worry about what we cannot control or change? We need just accept and deal with each situation, knowing there is a loving higher force and helpers at each shift and turn in the road. At the end of a physical life, we will travel through a tunnel that connects the physical life with spiritual life and continue to be connected to all that is, was, and will be.

It appears to me upon further observation that the world of Spirit resides in a concentric circle bordering very closely to our own physical world. It is possible these dimensions of energy mix and penetrate as they swirl in the energy force that is the essence of all life in the cosmos. Psychics and mediums are highly sensitive to these energies and are involved in this continuing collaboration between spirits and humans.

Sometimes, in the most unexpected ways, we find
angels at our disposal right here on earth.

CHAPTER 21
Children of One Source

"The simple things are also the most extraordinary things, and only the wise can see them."
Paulo Coelho, *The Alchemist*

After lunch, I proceeded to St. Francis Hospital to clarify a dispute between several insurance companies over who was obligated to pay the bill for an operation my husband had had two years ago. My husband felt if I went to the office at the hospital, I could get a letter in writing saying we were not responsible. The insurance company approved the procedure prior to the surgery and now repeatedly was sending us a bill. I parked and had a long walk past the chapel, finally arriving at the main lobby. A receptionist told me that Mercy Hospital near my home took care of this type of billing, and I had come all the way across Long Island to the North Shore. She pointed to the cashier's office and told me perhaps I could get some assistance there.

A lovely young woman gave me a phone number and told me to use the phone outside her cubicle. I followed the telephone instructions and was finally connected to Janet. I mentioned how another Janet had originally connected me to the talented medium John Edward, and she was eagerly excited to talk about intuitive readings. Janet said that she and her sister would love a reading, as they had just lost their father. Perhaps she would like to try a session in my office? She gave me her address and asked me to send some information.

Then I told Janet about the ongoing fight over my husband's surgery bill. Janet responded that she would call and get that situation resolved. I was so grateful for her expertise and help and felt comforted by Janet's description of what would be done while confident of a positive outcome.

From there, I proceeded to the hospital gift shop. I love hospital gift shops. They often have great, well-priced items. I picked two pumpkin, chocolate marshmallow candies and went to pay for them. I then noticed the children's books and purchased a version of *Peter Pan* that I liked. I was anxious to leave but was delayed long enough to hear a woman talking about her son who had moved to Switzerland. I had a thought only the other day that Switzerland might be a civilized place to visit or maybe even live. Her son had been somewhat wild and then had met a Swiss girl. They dated over the summer, and when she returned to teach in Switzerland, he visited her. They got married, and his company made it easy for him to be transferred to Switzerland. Spirit does intercede even when we might not be aware of their divine help.

She went on to tell me her name was Joanne and said she was happy with her boyfriend of 12 years and had been married to another man for 32 years. Her boyfriend was interested in Kabbalah and Jewish tradition, though he was not Jewish. Sometimes personal interests are generated from soul memories and may seem out of sync with the life and family we are presently connected to. She was aware that Kabbalah believed names and dates appeared to be codes towards living the life that we were born to experience and could be connected to past lives. Joanne then remarked that her son Tommy, who was in Switzerland was born on 11/7, and I said that was the day my mom died, and then she said his son was christened on 10/26, and I announced that was my father's birthday. She also told me her boyfriend was born on 7/14, and those were the days of my mother's and my father's deaths. We agreed it was very pleasant for us to have met and to have shared our remembrances of soul and Spirit.

I enjoyed hearing Joanne's delight in telling me about her boyfriend, the closeness that they shared, and the respect they had for Judaism and Catholicism. I noticed that people who had more knowledge about the similarities of religions were happier and living better lives. A nagging, relentless feeling and thought of mine for some time now requires that all religions will and must merge together, as they should never have been separated. The conflicts in the world that continue to escalate, causing loss of life and creating continuous world disasters, are based on the failure of our evolving thoughts to more realistically understand and embrace religion and life, appropriately bringing about a clearer new view and modern take on past traditional religious stories and fundamentalist views. The woman behind the counter called to a nun who was from St.

Francis Hospital. The nun walked in with a smile and touched my shoulder. She was a spiritual healer and remarked that she was aware that I was also. This reminded me of my trip to Italy: While in Italy, I had stood in front of St. Francis's church. There was a statue of St. Francis with three doves around his head. As you know, three doves were the message my mother promised to send me from the afterlife. At that moment I had an epiphany. If each of us could walk in the spirit of good saints and good souls by raising our consciousness to small moments of great kind intentions, how the world would be illuminated. Nuns, saints, and mothers all at this moment seemed to me as teachers of the virtues of a fine soul existence.

David and I were off to visit Las Vegas for a short trip and we were sitting in different rows on the plane. I never questioned my seating, as I knew there were no coincidences, and I would be in the right spot to share a soulful moment with someone. I was seated next to Alfonso and Ginny, both in their late 60s, and both had lost their spouses. They had been friends for the past six years. Alfonso was a pharmacist, and I mentioned my dad was a podiatrist and his good friend Mac a pharmacist. Alfonso mentioned his marriage had lasted 43 years, and he had 11 grandchildren.

Alfonzo did believe something survived physical death; however, he still missed his first wife.

I wanted to try a little experiment, so I told him I would shut my eyes and see if there was a message from his wife in Spirit. I took a deep breath and asked for something from Spirit to help him. Immediately I felt myself on a large cruise ship looking down at the moving water. I saw cliffs and islands jutting into the water, quite like the magnificent view I had been so delighted to see when visiting Greece on cruise. I asked Alfonso if he had gone on a cruise with his wife. "Oh, no," he answered. "She was afraid of the water, and so is Ginny." Well, I was surprised since the image was so clear. What could it mean? In a few minutes, he said, "I always wanted to go on a cruise, but I couldn't talk Rosie into it. Now I can't go with Ginny either." I imagined Rosie was letting him know she was sorry she didn't go with him on a cruise and held him back from that amazing experience. Then I spoke to Ginny about how great my cruise to the Greek Isles had been, hoping to spark in her a desire to have an adventure while she was still young and healthy enough to do it. Maybe the message from Alfonso's first wife was just a simple impression, perhaps a way to say, "Hello, darling. I am still with you in love, and have a wonderful cruise."

Rabbi Priest and An Interfaith Service

As a result of seeing an article in the local *South Shore Record*, which was on top of a pile of magazines at my office, I became aware that Temple Israel in Lawrence, where my son had his bar mitzvah years before, was holding an interfaith service.

I remembered telling the rabbi there that it was becoming clear to me that psychic mediums could retrieve messages from Spirit and these messages helped loved ones deal more effectively with loss and develop a greater love for life. I was more aware now that my love for God or life, since I was a child, seemed to be a philosophical remnant of my Jewish ancestral heritage and also a need to connect as an intuitive to the spiritual unseen world to help others know, navigate, and fulfill planned destinies. We were connected to our ancestors throughout time and space, not alone as so many people thought.

I also told him that many of the structured religions seem to teach an exalted, prejudicial love for their own group and create feelings of superiority while putting others at a disadvantage for their personalized, and at times different, religious beliefs. Religion has, in my estimation, traveled far from the simple beliefs of the olden-day Jews, who believed in a loving, yet at times commanding, God of praise, promise, and brotherhood. Others may have seen God as a force to swiftly correct the evil deeds of men, but I only see and feel the energy of life as benevolent and kind. Much of world dissension and wars have been fought in the name of God, but more often it was to procure and allow their church, temple, or group to hold more power over their congregations. Much of the divisiveness we are seeing in America and the world at large these days, is a result of the way politicians plan and work for securing the rights and needs of their constituency, and separating, rather than unifying, their nations. The pain of these relationships must be given up for more interactive processes, and Spirit will, in these changing times, insist on equality of men and women, black and white, Jewish, Christian, or Islam and will insist on groups meeting to find common ground. It is not a request from Spirit but a Divine Decree for the healing of our earth population.

A thought flashed through my mind. I remembered that as I sat in temple as a young girl, I giggled at the chanting by the men and felt they appeared robotic in their murmurings. Then I remembered before Gregg's bar mitzvah that I received a call several months before the scheduled event from the temple, and they told me he was not going to be able to be included in the service, as he hadn't learned his Haftorah. Obviously, he was like me, unsettled or unimpressed with the structure and rigidity of the system. Maybe like me, he had a need to include everyone—Jew, Gentile, or any other religious or cultural belief system—into the mix of our human brotherhood. He did eventually settle down and have his bar mitzvah, but as was true to his nature and life plan, he went into the world to learn about many different kinds of people, rejecting separation and limited thinking.

Now Gregg and Lea have three beautiful sons—Sullivan, Greyson, and Graham—and when I visit them in California, the boys run to me with such openness of heart and love and hug me and their brothers, telling me, "This is my bru-tha." We should all remember the brotherhood of humanity and the authenticity of real love for each other past the limitations of ancient religions and political laws made by men, not God.

The rabbi had strongly suggested, when I told him about my healing practice and messages from Spirit, that I study Torah or Kabbalah and should not be as interested in psychics or mediums. I was slightly miffed by this suggestion, as I was happily proceeding along my spiritual path and was meeting many noted mediums and energy healers who were empathic and had great humanitarian will.

Now years later and for the first time in the history of Temple Israel in Lawrence, a bishop from the Diocese of Rockville Centre was delivering a sermon on the High Holy days, and this historic interfaith event was put into motion by the rabbi I had spoken to years before. In my estimation, a spiritual leader must address and conquer the issue of prejudice that is harbored knowingly or unknowingly in many hearts. Then it will be possible to reach out to brothers and sisters of all faiths with love, respect, and a spirit of goodwill so the true words and feelings of God can be honored.

I believe that people who have the gift of mediumship
are called by God to serve and any way one finds God
or the Universal Source of Life is the right way.

In studying Kabbalah, which is at least 4000 years old, 2000 years before Christ's time, I found that beliefs in an afterlife, angels, and the concept of life after death were first Jewish concepts, not Christian revelations as I had thought. In fact, Christianity is but a continuation of Judaism with several additional messages from Jesus, an enlightened gifted soul of enormous energy and talent, a healer, possibly a medium, and of course, as we all are, a beloved child of God. Christianity uses many symbols of other religions, including Judaism.

In John 14:12, John says, "I tell you the truth, anyone who believes in me will do the same works I have done, and even greater works, because I am going to be with the Father."

In dreams and meditation these very words come to me.

"Truly I say to you, what I do, you shall do and more." I think Jesus either wished for or foresaw a time when people would individually connect to their own divine energy and many, or all, would communicate with Spirit.

Matthew tells us, "Be ye therefore perfect, even as our Father God which is in Heaven is perfect." I believe this means seeking the highest good in others and ourselves. While we will never be perfect in the physical world, we can access the divine quality of God within us and strive towards our own personal growth, higher awareness, and love.

When I read this article, I was happy the rabbi and priest were making a stand for peace and bringing together the Catholic and Jewish faiths, as I believe they are one and the same except for cultural and minor regional traditions.

It would be one of my fondest hopes for all people
of God to live more fully in love and become evolved
children of the Universe while here on Earth.

CHAPTER 22
Mediums Are Sensitive as Children

It is because I think so much of warm and sensitive hearts
that I would spare them from being wounded.
Charles Dickens, *Oliver Twist*

It was Saturday, and before I left for the office, I remembered I was going to one of the most expensive French restaurants in New York City, Alain Du Casse, in the Essex House on Central Park West. I had already decided on a sleeveless, black sheath dress and big strands of pearls that had been in the top drawer of my chest since my children were little. It seemed that the classic styles of the past and quiet elegance appealed to me, much like learning the simplicity of the laws of energy. In digging into the back of my drawer for a pair of black nylon stockings, I discovered a large box that I hadn't been aware I was missing. I was delighted to find a small marcasite heart with the Star of David that my grandmother gave to me when I was a little girl. She had also given one to each of my four cousins and my two sisters. I had been thinking of this necklace recently after seeing my cousin Susan wearing hers and had no idea where it was and so wished to find mine. I loved this necklace, especially because it was from my grandmother Sarah, from whom I never heard a harsh word. She loved food, jewelry, her family, and the United States. As an immigrant from Russia, she appreciated the freedom and opportunities for herself and her children. She had never owned a home but had a lovely apartment in an old building in Brooklyn. My aunt's uncles and cousins were there each Sunday, eating and laughing with such abandonment. Perhaps my grandmother Sarah had a little Susan energy that kept her close to her home and family, and that was enough for her.

Personally, I had been exposed to many more worldly opportunities and had assumed responsibilities so different from my training and the values instilled in me from my earlier beginnings and my immediate family. My greater reach outward to people other than my family would have seemed so alien to my family. In pursuit of spiritual awareness and enlightenment, I had come to recognize responsibility for the world's people and interests far beyond my original intentions.

Everything changes as we grow and assume responsibility for
seeing beyond the immediate reality to the possibilities that exist.

❖

I believe more and more people will be made spiritually aware through personal experiences or through world events. Little by little, step-by-step, God will awaken this present-day group of mortals to the reality of the next dimension and to their real purpose for life on earth. Spirit may begin with the children and lift them up to hold their own sense of goodness and help the elders be more aligned to their own innocence. In fanning and cooling the rage and anger of these modern times, miracles will be seen more often, and kindness and love will be shown to those experiencing life-threatening traumas who will, at times, be saved and then express their love of life. Healers and those in Spirit who constantly offer divine intervention will awaken a sensitivity of hope and gratitude towards the spiritual workers who are walking with us and sharing our sorrows as we move towards greater love, happiness, and awareness of our divine nature.

I suddenly realize while reading the above words written years ago that in the reading recently received from Spirit, they are nearly the same words. Maybe the angels were validating for me that I have been fulfilling my life destiny by sharing these thoughts in word and action all my life. What is true and right comes to us over and over again until we know in our hearts who we are, how connected we are to Source, and how we will eventually improve the collective reality of the world.

True Acceptance of God and Nature

I rushed home and dressed for dinner, telling David the story of the day. For the first time in a while, he responded in a positive way to my spiritual enthusiasm. "You are not the story; you are the messenger." I often told him that, but it had not been easy for him to accept the changes in my reality and life. I wasn't, David says, a medium when he met and married me, but indeed I was a medium always, just not fully aware or ready to begin that part of my spiritual journey until the time was right. Ultimately, it was not a loss of attention to him or others but my need to be involved with many new people and expressions of this spiritual aspect of life. It reminded me of the movie I often watched at Passover when Miriam, wife of Moses, said to the daughter of Pharaoh, who also loved Moses, "You lost him when he went to seek his God. I lost him when he found him." If we follow a purposeful life plan, we discover and hopefully fulfill our destiny, though not everyone will be comfortable with certain choices made. Unconditional love is then more than love for one person, family, self, or even God but the full range of goodness that radiates in intensity throughout the soul to others.

David and I proceeded to the city and met Stacey and Jeremy for a drink at a plush bar. They both looked so happy. Youth and love are a beautiful sight. They left, and we made our way in traffic to the restaurant, where we met friends from early college and law-school days. It had been quite a while since we had been out together. I tried in the course of the discussion to disclose something that was relevant to my work. I mentioned that I was able to give my clients accurate images and impressions about others in their daily life and also for those who had passed. These impressions seemed to come from deceased friends or family members and gave a more insightful understanding of situations they had shared in life. The information was very helpful to understand how to improve themselves and any troubled relationship. While some messages were not earth-shattering, many messages did clarify relationships that were strewn with misunderstandings and miscommunications. My husband's friend blasted me and said, "Sheryl, enjoy your life now. There's nothing else." So, it seemed that everyone did not share my excitement about knowing that life survives this life. Finally, after years of enthusiasm to share messages from Spirit, I am learning that I cannot always do so.

I mentioned that my son, Gregg, was dating a girl from Sweden. My friend asked if she was Jewish. She obviously was not Jewish. My friend told me how the Jewish people were still the holders of God's light. I couldn't restrain myself and I responded, "You know, those kinds of thoughts were our parents' way of seeing that we stayed in our own selective breeding pool. Also, maybe those thoughts were a way to encourage us to procure higher education and success in the materialistic world. It is, in essence, an untruth. There are many untruths I have had to shed in this time of spiritual growth. Every group has gifted and intelligent people, and in every group, there are those at a lower form of functioning. There is no one better race or religion, here or in heaven. In the next dimension, each soul is honored and respected and part of the whole tapestry that is God's perfection." She became quiet for a moment, and while I am sure she might not yet be able to embrace what I said, I am glad I no longer limit myself in judgment or in choice of friends or experiences according to the narrowness and rigidity of a mindset given to me and others in the early days of our lives.

In reflecting on the discussion of the evening, I realized that sometimes more evil than good has been done in the name of God throughout history. Nature, both human and of the physical world, gives us, through normal but sometimes harsh realities, much of the pain and suffering we internalize. God is the Creator and Provider of unconditional love while nature is the process of a physical life that must have a beginning and an end. Both offer great possibilities for our soul world.

After a late night of indulging in too much food and champagne, I knew I would have difficulty getting up for my yoga class. It was nine o'clock in the morning, and David said, "Aren't you getting up?"

"I can't. I'm too tired." David went downstairs for breakfast, and I kept my eyes closed. Soon I heard in my thoughts, "Get up, lazy bones." I looked at the clock. I still had time to make the class if I hurried. When I got to yoga, I noticed this pretty, golden-haired young woman who was wearing a purple workout shirt. I especially liked the color on her. This girl reminded me of a young woman I had recently met at my office who said to me that I might not be meant to give psychic readings to lots of people, just to select people. Being quite intuitive herself, she told me she had lost her mother when she was only twelve years old. I always felt sad to hear that a young person had lost a close relative so early in their lives. I considered myself most fortunate to have had my mother, father, and grandparents with me to experience many important milestones in my own life.

My yoga instructor was not there but the class was in full swing and was an excellent stretching workout. At the end of the activity I was putting my sneakers on when the young girl with the blonde hair sat down next to a girl near me. She started to mention that she was starting a new job after a year's search. Her company had folded after ten years. She said she had been meditating a lot in the hopes she would adjust to the new job. Actually, she was worried. I jumped in and said, "I am somewhat intuitive, and I sense you will do quite well." We introduced ourselves, and she told me that she had lost her mother three years before. Her father had died when she was a little girl. Even though she had suffered such a double loss in her early life, I sensed great acceptance, spirituality, and capacity to love.

As she drove away, I thought what a coincidence that I had recently met two young women who looked alike and who had both had the loss of mothers and fathers in their lives. Was it a coincidence that I was there to encourage them when their mothers were not?

Faith, Destiny, and Our Life Plan

I recently paid a condolence call to a family and friends who had lost a young female member. She had passed after many years of battling a serious illness. I found myself talking to the rabbi, who had delivered a most memorable service. We talked about Spirit and my belief of the survival of the soul. I think he was in tune with my vibration and belief system. The rabbi said he had lost his mom, dad, and brother and felt their closeness often. Then he said something that others might have thought strange. "This young woman didn't die because she was being punished for anything."

"Of course," I said. "We all come with a life plan. Many experiences and challenges seem designed for the benefit of one's soul development, and people crossing our path are not there randomly. I am convinced we are all interconnected and we are mirroring attitudes and behaviors leading us to eventually make changes to refine any negative thoughts or actions. Those who are unable to explore their inner thoughts or accept responsibility for what they are creating in their life may experience more conflict and difficulties while those people acting in more loving and thoughtful ways towards others would seem to elevate to a higher consciousness and provide a kinder sharing of life.

But try as one may, changes happen, and the forces of nature and physical environment can create havoc, disease, or death and challenge us. I prefer to call this faith, destiny, and our life plans. There are no accidents or coincidences in any of our lives. There are, however, tests or events designed to improve our acceptance of a higher energy or God and, of course, a grand plan for each of us.

After speaking with the rabbi, I happened to be standing next to a young woman with curly, sun-streaked hair. I noticed her sparkling blue eyes and remarked that she resembled a cousin of mine named Susan, who had just moved to New Jersey. This young woman seemed to be a wise, spirited girl. We enjoyed talking about my energy healing work and the book I was working on. She seemed so open and aware of these metaphysical principles. It is often hard for people to believe there is a God or loving divine energy when there seems to be so much pain and misery in the world. I believe physical life is determined by natural processes and is part of a process of duality reflecting good and bad. Life has been created with all its beauty, in all its fragility, so that we can experience the full range and balance of all emotions and energies.

Somehow, I mentioned to this young woman that I had been receiving many young women in her age range, 30 to 40, who were either having difficulty getting pregnant or wanted to get pregnant in a certain time frame but were not married yet and were fearful.

The young woman's face turned white, and she said, "This is very strange, but I am hoping to have children and I am unmarried. I planned to use artificial means to have a pregnancy. I wish to be a single mom." Years ago, I personally would've thought this not to be the best choice. It is a hard road to raise children, much harder in a single-parent family. Today, I understand that the choices we make and the destiny we follow will be accomplished one way or another even if considered untenable by others.

Life and birth are a continuous circle of fading in and fading out, from being born and living, from coming and going into different experiences and awareness of our energetic presence.

CHAPTER 23
Teachers, Practitioners, and Spiritual Leaders

There is a reason they call God a presence - because
God is right here, right now. In the present is the only
place to find Him, and now is the only time.
Elizabeth Gilbert, *Eat, Pray, Love*

Scheduled to host a Reiki demonstration at a local library, I was in my office preparing when quite suddenly, a small boy, Michael, who was scheduled to see one of the therapists, walked boldly into my office. Michael was about eight years old, and he was early for his appointment with the occupational therapist. Michael asked if he could stay with me, as his bus driver had dropped him off early and neither his mom nor the therapist was there yet. We started to read a story together. He hugged me and thanked me for letting him hang out, and he asked when he could have a Reiki session with me. I thought that perhaps Reiki would help ground him and help him develop better concentration. He was very intelligent and also sensitive.

Later, his mom, Barbara, came in to my room and thanked me for letting him stay with me until his teacher had arrived. Barbara had taken Michael for yoga sessions, which had seemed to calm him. Michael also took karate classes with Robert Hansen, who is a psychic medium. I had been to his karate studio for a demonstration of mediumship recently. Robert Hanson had been a special education teacher, as I had been, and he had an autistic son.

Michael soon became a regular Reiki client and was most respectful of the time we spent together. At some point, he let me know it was now time to call him Mike. It was not a coincidence, in my opinion, that Michael—I always call people by their full name in my thoughts—was led to two different and distinct healers to advance his adjustment to the world and to best deal with issues related to autism. It seemed we were all connected for some purpose.

It became apparent to me after working with Michael that his levels of anxiety, sensitivity, and fear were greatly diminished and his level of confidence continued to escalate. I believe Reiki sessions and learning the science and art of energy healing could help many children and adults dealing with autism, anxiety, or other sensory issues.

A few days later, I was at a hospice facility in Glen Cove where I volunteered my services. It seemed I kept ending up in Glen Cove, which was not close to my work or home. Recently, I went to a health spa in Glen Cove and was not sure what kept pulling me to that area. Perhaps certain areas, it seems, have stronger energy for the development of one's psychic abilities. The massage therapist at my office told me that three important mediums came from that area, and while they were no longer living, perhaps their spiritual energy lived on in that area.

On this particular day, a rabbi was scheduled to speak in the lunchroom of the Glen Cove health facility I visited. His sermon was exactly what I am attempting to relay through my writing. "There is a miraculous God who keeps this wondrous world functioning. The sun rises and sets; night comes as does the day; and we are never alone. All is in its place. Sometimes we upset the balance and forget how truly fantastic this life can be." In the past, I had heard another young rabbi speak. Today, from his appearance and his voice, I could tell this was the father of the young rabbi who always visited the care center. Both men, son and father, were rabbis. How sweet.

❖

Saturday night, I went to a college production at Marymount Manhattan College, where I was pleasantly amazed by the talent of the young performers. A friend's daughter was performing in a play, *The Adding Machine*, by Elmer L. Rice at the Theresa Lang Theatre.

The college ensemble performed Elmer Rice's play, which was written in 1923. The main character, a man named Mr. Zero, had worked as a bookkeeper for 25 years. He was uninspired by his home life, his marriage, and his work. He was fired and told by his insensitive boss that a high-school student and an adding machine would replace him. He lost control and stabbed the man with a bill holder.

Fleeing the scene of the murder, he returned home, where his wife yelled at him for being late and informed him that friends were arriving shortly. There were five couples invited for the evening, and their names were Mr. One, Mr. Two, Mr. Three, and so on. The people were nameless and lost in their dismal lives. Boredom and a misunderstanding of what life and joy were really about prevailed. In short order, two policemen arrived and removed Mr. Zero, who eventually was tried found guilty and executed.

In Act II of this play, this man rose from his grave to talk with another man who had also been executed for murdering his mother. Both men had felt the pain and shame of their short lives but were unable to know what to do in this afterlife. They sensed there was music to hear in this otherworldly place but didn't know what would activate the sound. After a while, they moved into the next setting or level in heaven and found themselves on a warm beautiful island.

Suddenly, Mr. Zero's assistant, an unmarried woman of meticulous composure, appeared. She was out of breath and running to catch up with him. He asked her how she had passed, and she said after he had been executed, she had committed suicide. It seemed she was in love with him all along. If things had been different, they might have discovered they were well-suited for each other. They talked of their undisclosed feelings for each other and began to dance. Their happiness was complete, and she wished to remain with Mr. Zero in this paradise. He faintly heard the music but felt, as he did in life, that he was not entitled to happiness and love and as a result, he ran from her. She realized she hadn't been able to be with him in life and couldn't be with him in death. Love, it would seem, or self-love, was the necessary ingredient to eternal life and the sounds of the Universe.

Without love, there is no joy, no music, no connection to the divine. Bring love into your life in all ways. Conquer despair, and you will bring love into the Afterlife.

❖

This play portrayed part of the theme of our spiritual journey. One of the messages I impart often to those who came to me for healing sessions was to recognize their co-creation with God's larger plan so we can be united in companionship with that divine energy of love. The virtues of love, devotion, integrity, honesty, joy, balance, harmony, dedication, and any other positive human emotion are what we are here on earth to gather unto ourselves. Connections to our fellow human beings, friends, neighbors, and family are what make life worthwhile.

CHAPTER 24
The Meaning of Relationships

*If you make your relationship with your Inner Being your top
priority, and you deliberately choose thoughts that allow your
alignment, you will consistently offer the greatest advantage
to others with whom you interact. Only when you are aligned
with your Source do you have anything to offer another.*

Esther Hicks

Just before Christmas, I walked into my office, put my purse down, and noticed a tissue and a napkin placed by three toy bears on my desk. I had not left the tissue or napkin. One of the three bears was a gift from my client, Mike. I picked up the tissue, and the musical bear started to play *Jingle Bells*. I had not been able to get it to play even when I touched the correct spot. It seemed like a setup...that a caring, absent friend or spirit arranged the tissue and napkin so the music rang out when I shifted the tissue. Was this a joke from Spirit? What did it matter? Friends were on vacation, and the office was quieter than normal. The music played and made me smile.

Later that day, I went to a store that always had holiday pieces that I purchased and added to my collectible village. I have always celebrated Christmas and Chanukah, as both holidays represent joy, freedom, and connection to Spirit. I also like to collect small items like boxes, figurines, and antique silver treasures.

For my Christmas village at home, I have gathered houses, offices, landmark buildings, stores, schools, hospitals, museums, theaters, bridges, parks, people, sporting arenas, and people engaging in work and play. Because I've gathered items of interest from all the exotic and cultural places I had traveled to over the years, it seemed each piece in the village represented a place I've visited, people I've worked with, family, friends, or meaningful experiences in my life. At the store, I saw a horse and carriage with a girl and boy, and the title on the box was, "Dashing through the Snow." I remembered the musical bear that played *Jingle Bells*, and I remembered there is a line in that song that says, "Dashing through the snow in a one-horse open sleigh." The thought of romance in a sleigh with a loved one hearing music together and moving through the holiday season with joy reminded me of the play I had just seen and how if we are not careful, we might lose the moment when love is right before us.

A Medium's Hunch

Sometimes it is sad for an intuitive person or medium to have foreknowledge about certain events, as certain events cannot be altered. Spirit not showing me everything about my own life or about those closest to me is something that is necessary. However, I have learned that life is always changing drastically for all of us, and I am acutely aware of the importance of God's guidance at all times, knowing that what is ultimately best for each soul while involved in their stories or dramas of love, family, honor, and trust is being played out as intended. These souls, my friends, and the characters who are the backbone of this book are in this life, attempting to learn new and improved ways to interact with each other.

Results with past-life regression sessions have brought me some awareness of several people who may have had Roman or Greek lives with me.

In a past-life regression, I sensed that it was in a Roman city where a protector, a soldier of high standing, said good-bye to me as he went off to war. This person, I felt, supported my choices in many lives and as a result of our interactions, helped me develop my own source of personal power and strength. At the time of that specific past-life regression, I visualized my beautiful son, Gregg, who was also my son in that ancient life in Rome.

In my travels, I met a Native American shaman who told me that I had a father figure standing over me protecting me and he had been with me many lifetimes: a guide a teacher an angel all are with us as we travel through the experiences of this life.

Most people desire to be in relationships to fulfill dreams or to be with a true twin soul. Words that resonate and express this sentiment for me are from Elizabeth Barrett Browning's famous poem *How do I Love Thee*: "How do I love thee? Let me count the ways. I love thee to the depth and breadth my soul can reach, and should God choose, I would but love thee greater after death." These words express the soul's divinity and for love in all relationships for all time.

Soul Mates

Last night I saw the movie *Cold Mountain*, a Civil War story involving a reference to romantic love. The love that ignites ever so briefly in this movie between a young woman of means and a working-class man before he was taken away to fight in the Confederate Army was intense and sudden. It seemed a true twin-soul connection. They were from different backgrounds but bound together through the atrocities of war and deprivation that invaded their lives. Their love surrounded them well beyond sustained torture and loss, and they were unexpectedly reunited briefly just before the end of the war.

However, one scene in the movie that related to the magic of spiritual messages that I am constantly downloading in my daily life, this Christmas and before, was made crystal-clear to me. In that particular scene, a neighbor asked the young woman to look into the water of a well through a looking glass. She received an intuitive impression of her beloved soldier walking towards her in the snow with several black ravens flying ahead of him. He seemed to be staggering. She had no idea what the image meant.

Many intuitions, impressions, or foretelling's are not understood until after the event. That is how it should be, for we cannot live in fear of the future. We must live in the moment and enjoy each timely experience. Knowing an outcome could taint the experience leading up to it. In the movie, her beloved soldier returned to her, and they consummated their love physically. They never had good timing before, but there was a moment that they could affirm their true feelings. Soon after their reunion, he was shot, and she saw him staggering towards her before he collapsed and died, just as she had seen in the vision in the water. She later discovered she was pregnant.

*Moments of true love, no matter how short or challenging,
are written in the eternal records of Divine Soul Energy.*

❖

Holiday Gifts

It was almost the night before Christmas. At work, I received a call from Tom, whom I hired to replace two stained-glass windows that had been destroyed in the upstairs level of my house. I have an English Tudor house that is almost 80 years old and have tried to retain its original workmanship and flavor, as its quaintness is uniquely beautiful. Several months ago, I spent hours with Tom selecting the pattern and the colors for the window. I wanted the replacements as close to the way the windows were when I purchased the house. Years before, two of the stained-glass windows were weak and buckling, and a glass man came. Instead of reinforcing and retaining the glass, he removed them. As I was not home at the time to stop this event, I was distressed and very unhappy with the ugly replacements. It bothered me for years, and finally I had the time and found the craftsman who could restore the windows. Tom had drawn a design of irises and butterflies.

Tom and I spent time talking about his psychic awareness and spiritual happenings. He shared stories with me of a place where he worked long ago, where he and the other workers, who stayed late at night, had seen people in spirit. In other words, the place was not only occupied by the living.

When Tom's dog got very sick, he was so busy caring for him that he didn't know when he could complete the job, so of course, I told him not to worry and that whenever he was able to come and install the new windows, I would be grateful.

Months passed, and just when I thought I should call Tom and find out how everything was going, I received a call from him saying the glass panels were ready. Tom had shown them to me in November when he completed them. The windows were gorgeous. However, he said unless we got a day when the temperature was over 50 degrees, he could not install them. The weather had been unseasonably cold, and we had already experienced two major snowstorms. It seemed that the windows would not be installed until the spring. Imagine how pleasantly surprised and delighted I was to receive Tom's call just before Christmas. The temperature was right, and he would be right over to install the new windows. I left the office and met him at the house. It was a powerful, beautiful Christmas and Chanukah miracle and brought much joy for me to have restored my English Tudor house to its original state.

Holidays with Neighbors

It was the weekend after Christmas. David was in Florida visiting his mother, and Margie, who had helped me in the house for years, had just flown to Ecuador after receiving a phone call that her brother had passed. Margie, the youngest of eleven children had lost her mom at an early age. Even though she had a strong Catholic background and believed in an afterlife, she was always greatly dismayed by the loss of anyone in her family, and her suffering was acute, which made it hard to offer much comfort. My knowledge of an afterlife has helped me with the passing of those closest to me. Feeling sadness at any loss, I have always realized the continuity of life and the plan that God has set in motion for each of us, and this is my saving grace. Each person's awareness of this reality is at a different level; therefore, grief and bereavement affect us all individually.

My entire family was away, and I was home alone when I received a frantic call from my neighbor Pat, who was having company and asked to use my oven.

Soon the husband of Pat's niece and Pat's son, Kenneth were knocking on my door. It was the first time I had met them, and he was so friendly. Both men were quite intrigued by the miniature holiday village in my living room, buildings spread out across several folding tables covered with soft artificial snow. We selected and placed each piece in a meaningful way, as it represented the progress of my understanding of life. Life is a work in progress, as was my village, showing continued stories of interconnected coincidences and meaningful lessons. The young man said he would return in a half-hour to pick up the warmed food. When he returned, he invited me to join them for dinner. I started to hesitate but then remembered a reading with Robert Brown in which I was told by my mother-in-spirit that often when I was invited places, I found excuses not to go and missed out on many creative opportunities. Since hearing that observation from a medium, which happened to be true, I have tried to graciously accept all invitations. Accepting the invitation, I got dressed and walked over to Pat's house.

Pat's house was decorated magnificently for the holiday, and Kathleen, Pat's niece, whom I'd known since she was a little girl, came over to say hello to me. Her new husband, I discovered, was half Jewish and half Catholic. He came to sit with me, and we began to discuss my new book, *Life Is No Coincidence*, which shared my newfound understanding over the course of the last five years that religious figures from all major religions had incorporated divine thoughts from the original patriarchal religion, Judaism, which was the first religion to accept that there was one creative divine source, or God. It might serve humanity's great expansion and evolution if all religions could be combined and infused with a spiritual point of view that there is only one, divine, loving energy force: God. The ever-surviving soul of each person reunites with all who have been or who will be again through God's energy of love. Kathleen's husband was quite intrigued, and I was amazed that as a lawyer, he could actually understand what I was saying. This young man was the product, and possibly the best representation, of both religious doctrines, Judaism and Catholicism, and was more open to the possibilities of universal energy. It was a wonderful party, and once again, Spirit brought people together who could share the magic of loving life.

❖

Children of Heavenly Energy

The other day, I had a Reiki session with a new client named Katherine. For some reason, I happened to mention that one of my clients was able to get pregnant via in vitro techniques and that client told me she felt her Reiki sessions had greatly supported the entire process.

Katherine responded, "I hope I don't get pregnant now. I'm past that time." We both laughed. As I began the session, I immediately sensed several spirits present. When I refer to a spirit, I think of a soul's eternal being that survives and still contains the individual qualities and personality of their former physical life. Spirits are just souls, life forces temporarily free of a physical body, so I can feel them present the same way I can sense and interact with a physical person. Spirit is any presence or life force from another dimension or afterlife. Two spirits were on one side of the family, and two spirits were on the other side. Katherine expressed that she had two close female relatives and two men in Spirit whom she hoped would still be together. Next, I sensed an abundance of green vegetation and asked if anyone on the other side liked gardening or had something to do with plants. Nothing came to Katherine's mind in that moment, but later in the reading, Katherine remembered her deceased uncle just mentioned had many plants sent to the wake. She was taking care of them and worried they would die. Katherine acknowledged those four souls that I had sensed were very important to her, and she was glad they were together in Spirit and still expressed their love for her.

Sensing her grandmother in Spirit, Katherine said that she had been gone a really long time. I told her that time didn't matter. Beyond this life there was no time. Loved ones came during a spiritual reading with love and assurances that they still existed and had not forgotten us. The next impression received was of hands holding a round object, and I asked if it was a religious picture or statue. It seemed she had a picture of Jesus holding a baby that her grandmother had given her, but now her sister had it. I sensed it was important to Katherine and asked if she might be able to get it back.

Then I observed a vibrant blue color and a male energy that was important to her, and I asked if she had a son. She responded that when she was having trouble getting pregnant, she had often touched the picture of Jesus that her sister had in her home now. One night, she had a dream that she was pregnant, and several days later, a baby boy was born. Katherine was able to adopt that child. Then I was flooded with tons of pink energy, and asked if there were girls in the family, many girls. Katherine said she had twin daughters and 13 nieces. Katherine also said she had gone for infertility treatments, and the result was her twin daughters born after her adopted son. "Funny," I said, "that I originally told you about the other clients who had trouble conceiving, and through faith, it happened for you. You also have achieved success in your own life through faith." I was most amazed at the effect the picture of Jesus had on Katherine's perception, and I believe that by accepting God's help, she surrendered her fears and healed her soul and body.

CHAPTER 25
Continuing to Learn and Expand

Knowing yourself is the beginning of all wisdom.
Aristotle

It was a chilly morning, and I was standing in front of a church in Manhattan waiting to attend a seminar presented by the Learning Annex. I was excited to attend this particular workshop featuring noted, metaphysical professionals from around the world, as I had especially wanted to hear Dannion Brinkley, who had experienced a near-death experience 25 years ago after being struck by lightning. Rosemary Althea, an English medium whose books I had read, was also going to present her story. Actually, there were seven speakers, and I was meeting Mike and his wife, Lois, friends from my weekly psychic development group.

I arrived a little early and was able to sit down on a damp outside bench to slowly enjoy my breakfast and drink an iced coffee. In a few minutes, a group of people gathered. They started to line up to enter the building. As I was finishing my drink, I went to stand behind Mike and Lois, who had just arrived, and noticed a tall dark-haired woman behind me. I only thought about this later, but why did I not talk to Mike and Lois? What prompted me to begin a conversation with this young woman? She was from Westchester. Her 83-year-old father had died last year. I mentioned that I was studying mediumship and believed some part of us survived physical death. I told her I was working on a book about life and an afterlife connection. Then I asked her name, and she responded Helen.

I asked, "Are you Greek?"

"Yes, and my family is from Sparta."

"How funny," I said. Several years ago, when beginning to practice meditation, my yoga teacher Pam gave me a tape to listen to. While following the meditation, I sensed and then heard the distinct words in a faraway voice say, "Helen...Troy." I don't know if that means I was that person in a life long ago or that Helen is my spiritual guide in this life. While on the other side, I may have shared experiences with her. It is possible that souls share experiences and can actually live them out through another person.

Perhaps I share a quality of the soul life of Helen of Troy experienced long ago. However, after hearing that name during meditation and among other references in dreams, I was able to take a trip to Greece. On the island of Rhodes, I had a tour guide named George who told stories of Helen of Troy. She had visited the island on her way back to Sparta after the ten-year Trojan War. Oddly enough, I bought the tour book and was disappointed not to find any mention of the information that George had given us, though he said the people had been very kind to Helen and appreciative of the golden bowl she had presented to them.

❖

We started to file into the church. The church was hot and muggy. There were tremendous rainstorms during the afternoon. The last several months had been one long, wet rain. I enjoyed listening to Michelle White Dove, a guest speaker from Colorado. She spoke of a near-death experience after a tragic car accident when she 18 years of age. She sensed in her inner thoughts that she should not go in the car with her friends that day but did not listen. Two blocks from the fatal crash, she changed seats with her cousin. He was instantly killed upon impact. She was most severely injured. During a near-death experience, she was out of her body. Spirit told her that she had work to accomplish and must return to her body. She responded, "You want me to go back to that broken body?" Given no choice, she returned to her body and suffered many months of pain and recovery.

Next Dannion Brinkley took the podium and described being pronounced dead for 28 minutes and the experiences he had during that time with beings of light. He wrote a book as a result of that experience, *Saved by the Light*. His sense of humor and presentation of the events were hysterical and very enjoyable, and he also discussed how 20 years of hospice work came about as a result of what he was told to do by Spirit. As a patient volunteer for hospice work, I was thankful to God that I didn't have to experience a near-death experience to put me in that place. Since

I am aware that our essence survives physical death, I feel obligated to help others deal with their fears and mistaken judgments about death and the dying process. Seeking to help the very young, the old, and the sick is to be as close to God as is humanly possible and what I truly try to honor. It may be the only way to learn compassion and love.

During a lunch break, we scurried to a café for a quick sandwich, as time was limited. When we returned, Dannion Brinkley was standing outside. I had so wanted to meet and talk to him and to tell him how I enjoyed his lecture, but I didn't really think there would be an opportunity to do this. Walking over there was a chance to tell him what a great teacher he was. He responded that after his near-death experience, he had returned to his life with a newfound intuitive ability to pick up a great deal of information about people when he held their hands or hugged them. Suddenly and unexpectedly, he hugged me and told me what a dynamic, vital person I was and that I was a pretty good teacher also. He autographed both of my books, and I hurried to my seat, as Robert Hansen was ready to begin.

Robert Hansen was a medium from Long Island, and I had been to a workshop at his karate studio recently. Robert Hansen began his presentation by saying that everyone who needed a reading would get one. There were a few hundred people in the audience. He began with an incident about a man who fell into the water from a boat. Another young man who was trained as a lifeguard jumped in after him. Both men drowned at Jones Beach. Robert was looking for someone on my side of the room, and actually he was standing close to me. I realized that last summer I had attended a child's birthday party in Huntington, New York. While waiting in line to get a painted tattoo with the kids, as I am sometimes very childlike and enjoy things just as much as the kids do, an adorable little girl said to me in a stern voice, "There is a line," and pointed to the back. I wasn't aware of the line and would just have waited until someone said it was my turn.

However, to appease the beautiful dark-haired little darling, I went to the back and sat on the ledge. Sitting next to me was the girl's mom, Donna. Her story unfolded. Perhaps my story of coincidences, our lives not being random, and my belief in an afterlife helped her to tell her painful story. It was her husband, a trained lifeguard, who had jumped in to rescue his father's friend, and both the men had drowned on the rocky shores of Jones Beach several months before. He was a volunteer fireman and had been at Twin Towers on September 11th, surviving that horrific day of mass destruction and death. Not long after, it appears, he had died in that boating accident.

Now here was Robert Hansen relating that story, but Donna was not part of my family. I didn't want to raise my hand and pull him to me if it was another family member who had drowned. I didn't respond. Someone on the other side of the audience tried to connect with Robert, but he was so sure he was with my side of the audience. Then he mentioned a podiatrist clipping toenails, and I jumped up and said that was my dad. Next Robert mentioned Bernadette Peters, who was in the Broadway show *Annie Get your Gun*, and he said something about a sharp shooter and a man who had had emphysema or died from a smoking-related disease. That was my first boyfriend, Ira. He had been a cowboy of sorts and owned a ranch out west. How funny that he came through with my dad and with the other young man who had drowned. Robert Hansen also mentioned that my mother was present, and her problem with her mouth had been handled wrong. She hadn't needed to have the surgery, which made her so unhappy. Gertie or Gertrude, a nickname for my aunt Gladys, was also mentioned, so I knew she was there also.

All in all, the information was accurate, and while there was no real message, there was proof showing that Robert indeed had impressions from the Spirit of my family members and Donna's husband.

Shortly after this event I received an invitation to the same child's party where I had met Donna. I would be able to give Donna the message that her husband was alive and well.

Here it was a year later, and as soon as I saw Donna, I quickly made my way over to her to tell her about my recent encounter with Robert Hansen, and was excited to tell her that her husband had come through along with my father and first boyfriend. As I looked at Donna's face when I said this, a thought went through my head: Donna's deceased husband had been her first love as Ira had been mine.

This thought helped me realize how intense, close, and profound the connection was. His death and the conditions surrounding it had been unbelievably hard for her, and my father had helped me make this connection of first love so that when I spoke to Donna, I could more compassionately understand her loss.

Donna had asked me a year ago if it was worth staying in this life with all its sickness and hardship, and instinctively, I had answered that I did believe life was a precious gift, no matter what the challenges were. Before my mom passed after a difficult three-month hospital stay, I remembered her saying, "Life was good. I have known love." Life, with all its difficulties, offers us relationships and the opportunity to know greater love. One can often find a moment of grace, courage, and love even in a time when so much seems to be lost.

I also remembered that a year ago I had told Donna that I sensed there would be another partner for her and a different kind of love. She was meant to experience first love: young love so she could know the closeness beauty and uniqueness of that special gift. After this loss, she would experience and know a different kind of relationship. She would experience a mature relationship of the soul. Every relationship, whether ended by divorce or death, was only meant to last as long as it did. No relationship is a failure, as all relationships are preparations for the next experience. This life journey is preparation for an Afterlife, and love, even when it ends unpleasantly, still registers in the greater energy of the Universe as love and is never lost. Before we parted, Donna told me she had met a wonderful man and was so happy to have this new friend.

❖

Coincidence in the Bronx

As has become evident to me over the last few years, wherever I travel, I meet people who are connected to me and share stories that bring us all closer together. No matter how far I roam from home, the parts of the puzzle are being brought together to fit.

David and I were leaving for Pennsylvania. Before going on our trip, David had to attend a closing at a real-estate office in the Bronx. As I watched David climb up a steep flight of old, cracked, marble steps, I decided I would walk in the neighborhood under the railroad trestle and find a place to eat. There was a Chinese place nearby. They did have a small table to hang out, and I began to read Dannion Brinkley's second book, *At Peace in the Light*. After an hour, I returned to the closing and sat down to wait for David to be finished. The real-estate agent who brought this deal to my husband sat down next to me. She was tall, with wavy dark hair, and wore sunglasses. She said she was having a problem with the iris part of her eye. I told her I was an energy healer and gave her my card. She soon told me her mother had died when she was twelve years old. They were driving in a car, and quite suddenly her mother pulled over to the side of the road. Her mother was only 32 years old, and she said to her daughter, "I will go to join my mother now," and she passed. Her grandmother had died three months before. We continued to talk. I said my mom had died on 11/7 and I met many people connected to these numbers, eleven and seven. She responded that her daughter Sarah was born on 7/11.

❖

We proceeded to Lords Way, Pennsylvania, where friends had a country house.

On Saturday, the rain flooded the roads in cascades of unending water. It appeared to me that God and his angels might be crying for all the unresolved anger and sadness in the world. As we have progressed technologically, it appears too many of us have fallen backwards, away from the basic humanity of a soul's understanding of love and small kindnesses. Fear, greed, hostility, aggressiveness, and anger have replaced the gentler side of life. In past times, family and community worked together for the safety and integrity of the system. Today, many people are carried along in a fast-moving chain of feelings, disconnected from those around them. We are absorbing too much stimuli, too quickly, and allowing our soul less interaction with our physical bodies. A disconnection of this magnitude is one of the causes of disease and dysfunction.

Disregarding the rain, my friend and I proceeded to Milford, a lovely, quaint shopping area. In the first store, I saw a metal door stop. It was a terrier dog, and it reminded me of a cute dog that belonged to my neighbor years before. Standing next to this dog was a cat doorstop. It reminded me that even these different species could cooperate and get along together.

I was looking for either a picture or some type of item related to Little Bo Peep, as the year before I had seen a Bo Peep water pitcher and had not bought it, as it was a bit overpriced. I remembered the little saying attached to the nursery rhyme for Bo Peep: "Little Bo Peep has lost her sheep and doesn't know where to find them. Leave them alone, and they'll come home, dragging their tails behind them." I remembered that my mother had dressed me in a costume of Little Bo Peep for Halloween one year and how she had enjoyed showing me that picture, which she'd saved. It seems we are all lost sheep in search of our true nature, and finding our true nature is the way Home.

Home, it would seem, is where the heart is. Home is where there is love and dedication, trust and faith, kindness and goodwill, and strength of purpose. Home, therefore, is where your soul- your higher self -reside. Home is in a good relationship or family or marriage where partners are not afraid of the growth and equality of the people around them. Where fragile egos exist and where there is restriction of the blossoming of the soul and the talents of another human being, there can be no peace or love. Always the search for home continues.

A woman directed me to a shop called *The Country Goose* down at the corner. The shop had an interesting mixture of both old and new items. There was a small children's section of cute items. I went to pay the woman as she wrapped breakable items, and immediately noticed a collection of photos on a shelf above her with an attractive young woman. In each picture there was a different celebrity, Barbra Streisand, Mel Gibson and others. I asked who the woman was. She responded, "That's my daughter Donna." I told her about the book *Life Is No Coincidence* that I was writing, showcasing the spiritual qualities that permeate our lives as we follow the grand design and distinct destiny created for us but also influenced by our choices and actions.

She mentioned that her husband had died several years before, and he was too young. She did not get messages from him and was angry that he had left her. We talked about my mom's near-death experience, and I explained how she had described the other side as being a place she could see herself going to and being happy. Somehow, I mentioned my mom had died on 11/7. The woman told me her daughter was born on 7/11. I handed the woman my card and told her during an energy healing session, I often received impressions and connections to those in Spirit. I invited her to visit me at my office should she travel out that way.

At that very moment, a young, attractive man in his early 30s with silver-gray hair and twinkling blue eyes walked into the shop. The owner knew him well and said, "John, please join us. We're talking about interesting stuff that you would like." John then said that he and his brother, Timothy, had just seen a medium on Long Island. They had just lost their father. Well, I remarked to John that in my book there were stories connected to the name Timothy. I proceeded to tell them a few of my Timothy stories, and then for some reason mentioned John Edward, a noted medium from Glen Cove, who had sparked an interest in my investigation and study of mediums. I had had my first psychic reading in Glen Cove and now did hospice work there. John then mentioned that his father had died in the Glen Cove Hospital. The three of us looked at each other, knowing that on this rainy day, three people were able to create a circle of light and bolster up feelings of hope and faith in the belief of an energy force stronger and more lasting than a fragile physical life could ever offer.

It would seem that home is wherever people share moments of love and an understanding of the divine Spirit of the Universe.

❖

Last week at a psychic development circle with Barbara, who was leading the group, only Steve and I were present. As we were three people, we sat and formed a triangle of energy. I thought it odd that there were only three people, as there were usually ten to twelve people at each workshop. Barbara said Spirit always arranged who was present and there were reasons for certain people being brought together.

Barbara mentioned that she sensed my Aunt Gladys in spirit, and she was being shown a gladiolus flower. The gladiolus flower, I later discovered, grows in all shades of the rainbow. Clusters of flowers grow on the side of the stem. If a cluster is cut, the flowers above them will open and continue to reach higher and higher. Spiritually, it would seem that my Aunt Gladys and Spirit were telling me I should continue my long climb without detours and might need to discard any old deterrents to this process.

Steve relayed several messages from Spirit that made me laugh. Steve said I had been in a small boat and had not thought about that for a long time. I only remembered two times being in small boats. Once when I was 16 and working for the first time at a sleep-away camp, I had gone in a rowboat with Ira. We were on a lake, and our paddle drifted away. I thought we'd never make it back to shore but at some point, realized while drifting, it was a great place to be alone in the silence and peace with the sun shining down on us. Ira was so laidback and relaxed. Time passed slowly and easily with him. One of the oars had fallen into the water. As I think back now on his laughing, sun-browned face, he probably knew all along he was able to get that oar back. He probably let it go on purpose to create a drama and become a hero in my eyes. But he was already a larger-than-life hero to me, being almost five years older. Tall, handsome, and strong in character and personality, he had a voice with a quality that could command your attention. At the same time, he could gently tease in a soft, endearing way. Having since that long-ago time learned that the soul can be seen not only by the eyes, but felt by the sound or tone of the voice, Ira was in every sense of the word, a loving mature soul. Since I seem to have had so many great connections to Greece at a time when people's innate intuitive sense was not an oddity but a standard part of life, that energy still resonates within me. Perhaps Ira and I were friends together at that time and place long ago.

The next time I was on a small boat was several years after the first experience. I had another unique experience. It was a dark cold night, and David took me to a friend's motorboat. My somewhat cautious or intuitive sense said we shouldn't go out in the dark on this dinky little boat. There were no lights on the boat, but not wanting to seem like a nerd, as David and his friends were older than I and extremely cool, I gave in to peer pressure and remained silent about my fears. Soon the boat's motor began to sputter, and then the engine died. We were drifting out to sea, and the lights from shore grew smaller and smaller. I was scared and annoyed that I hadn't followed my own intuition or gut feeling and had gotten into this dangerous situation. The guys tried to get the engine to work many times. It was cold, and the ocean waves were spraying all over us as we bumped back and forth on the choppy sea. Each time the engine refused to start; my heart sank deeper into dismay. I could see the headline, "Brooklyn College Sweethearts Lost at Sea." There was no peaceful or joyful excitement on this boat ride. They finally did get the engine to start, and we thankfully returned to shore. In that moment of finding our way back to shore, David was a hero and we were safe again. Some adventures, while holding unknown energy or not knowing the outcome, are still necessary for the soul to venture past the ordinary, in order to find the extraordinary and champion the feelings of fear. This night ended successfully, and we were all laughing as we left the boat. In retrospect, when one is in a comfort zone and not venturing into the unknown, they may not realize their full potential or soul needs, and relationships, like all events in our life, are overseen by the Divine, as we are led to the right places, partners, and practices that will heal the soul, even when we sometimes in our human thoughts do not see the full benefit of that Divine arrangement for us.

Then Steve spit out the words, "What's the deal with Spider-Man?" I had to laugh. Several weeks ago, at work, I had found a small, motorized action figure sitting on a small motorcycle and thought it was Spider-Man, but it was another action figure.

After this recollection, I decided to rent the Spider-Man movie. As I watched the movie, a very important love story unfolded. The heroine was Mary Jane, and the hero was Peter Parker. Mary Jane was the gorgeous strawberry-blonde with somewhat low self-esteem due to her home life and her emotionally uninvolved parents. Peter Parker was the quiet, shy underachiever. Because of her own family problems, she was unaware of Peter Parker's feelings for her. She was also unaware of her own potential and her own abilities. They both seemed to be stunted in their emotional development.

Bitten by a super-powerful hybrid spider, Peter soon went through a strange and wonderful physical transformation, but his spiritual transformation had a long way to go. This ordinary young man became a physical power to be reckoned with. When Peter's changes became obvious, his Uncle Ben became concerned about how Peter would utilize his gifts, and he said these very powerful words to him, "With great power comes great responsibility."

The love story between Peter and Mary Jane unfolded, and as is true of many great love stories, they cannot always end happily ever after. However, love experiences are necessary for the growth of our souls. We may wonder how, with all these increased technological advances, we seem still unable to harness and communicate our most loving feelings and move forward to create our best reality.

All of us have natural talents and gifts, and it is the use of these gifts that creates music, literature, art, and science, and all that make life in a physical world so grand.

CHAPTER 26
People Asking for Connections

Getting over a painful experience is much like crossing monkey bars. You have to let go at some point in order to move forward.
C.S. Lewis

On an unconscious soul level, we may accept the need for change, but our conscious level, or ego, jumps in and makes human maneuvers to control situations, which often hinders both our physical and soul lives. Why does this happen? The answer is fear! We are our own worst enemies. Everyone is at times guilty of this.

Therefore, we must not make any judgments about other people's behavior and actions, and we must not interfere in the way they choose to conduct their lives. At the same time, we must not allow others to make decisions for us and take away our personal power. Detachment from judgment and a greater expression of love towards those suffering the most can help them to find a way past pain to joy.

It was months since David and I drove to Lords Valley, Pennsylvania, and we had returned. I was at one of the surrounding small, quaint towns, and the first store I arrive at has a massive display of comic books. Being intrigued lately with Spider-Man and other superheroes, I asked the lady if she had any Spider-Man comics. She responded that she did and brought me a gigantic box. While browsing through the box, I saw a 1940 magazine with a loving couple on the cover. Inside the magazine, there were pictures of young soldiers. I realized that this was a magazine from before World War II. I carried the magazine with me to the rear of the store, and then my eyes fell upon a thin camel suede book with gold letters entitled *The Essence of Friendship*. I picked it up and hoped it wouldn't cost much. It was very hot in the store, and my friend left to wait for me outside. While I was paying for the Spider-Man comic book and the book about friendship, I noticed the Spider-Man comic book was entitled *The Web of Spider-Man*. David was always telling me I was like a spider, catching new people and dragging them into my web of stories of coincidences and synchronicity. I decided not to take the 1940 magazine and save some money, but the woman, whose name was Barbara, told me she wanted to give it to me. How nice! I thanked her and told her I was writing a book about coincidences and how there really are none. There are only events and people we meet who help us to realize we are either human beings having a spiritual life or perhaps spiritual beings having a human life. Barbara then told me that today was her birthday, and she was happy to give me a present.

It was hotter than I could remember. The weather should have been cooler here in the Poconos. Driving back to my friend's house, deer and turkeys, trees and green landscape were visible through the car window, alive with movement and life. Returning to the house, we turned on the air conditioner, and we both grabbed a cool drink. I sat down to look at my new book on the essence of friendship, a beautiful book from 1910, and each page was like a lithograph, with green and red borders of flowers surrounding the beautiful writings of great masters on thoughts about friendship. Happy to be sharing this book with others who had read and enjoyed it in days gone by, I finished reading it, and when closing it, I noticed that on the front page, the man who had owned it inscribed it. His name was Myron. My father's name is also Myron. The handwriting of the name almost looked like my dad's handwriting. My father, Myron, wasn't kidding when he said he was collaborating on writing this book with me.

There are patterns and meaning to all things in heaven and earth, and for each human, there is a series of events to guide them to face fears and negative thoughts and, with help from loved ones, to turn fear into beauty and love. This was truly what a spiritual being having a human experience was supposed to be about. The spiritual being transforms the human experiences and has a spiritual experience that will increase the soul's vibration and perfect whatever unloving fearful urges remained. It is a continuous and difficult procedure for most people. Really, it now seemed to me to be the major purpose of our earthly experience.

Right after the Pennsylvania trip, I returned home and went as is my usual routine to my nail salon. I had met many people of different back-grounds, religions, and races there. I felt it was a place of healing, as any place where people who work on the body and share energy often help others open to peace and healing. It is when the body and mind quiet that healing might occur.

At the salon, I sat next to a woman who said she had a dear friend since childhood, and they had seen each other through many challenging times. I responded that I thought it was no coincidence that she had such a wonderful friend. Perhaps they had decided to share this journey and lifetime together even before they were born. They might have made a promise to be there for each other and to bolster each other up no matter what and also to share the many joys of this life.

From the moment we are born, our life story has partially been written. Our lives already include many of the experiences and people who will interact with us. During these interactions and growth periods, our free will enables us to make decisions. We each decide how we will deal with the situations that confront us, either growing in soul strength and character through thoughtful, loving decisions or regressing through negative, destructive decisions. The game plan is already there in place, but the way we play the game—either by helping teammates or establishing roadblocks in their path or our own path—is our individual choice. Since I believe something survives physical death and that this is not the only life experience we have had or will have, I believe there are great possibilities and plenty of time for individual awareness and growth and for the collective growth of the general population.

At that moment, the woman I was speaking to announced, "I have lost two daughters, and I know they are always around me." My stomach dropped, realizing the sorrow generated by that statement, and I was in that moment so glad she had told me she had a close and wonderful friend. When I regained my balance, I responded, "They are absolutely near to you."

I then told this woman a few of my spiritual stories about connections to those in Spirit, and then she asked if she might tell me one of her own. I am often amazed that people share their intimate, loving stories. I am not quite aware what I say or do that allow this to happen. Perhaps I just seem like a warm, safe energy of tolerance, hope, or love. Her story began with a trip to a framing store to do an errand for her boss. While there, she saw a beautiful 5 x 7 frame and felt compelled to buy it even though she didn't know what picture would go in it. It was Christmas time, and her son-in-law visited her that very evening. He had recently lost his wife, who was this lady's daughter. When he arrived, he handed her a 5 x 7 picture of her and her deceased daughter lovingly touching each other's face. He said, "I didn't have time to get a frame." She responded that she bought a frame that very same day, and it was the perfect size for this perfect picture. When I asked the lady her name, she said, "Roseanne."

Roseanne said that she looked forward to reading my book *Life Is No Coincidence*. Her belief in God and her belief that she would see her daughters again sustained her. One of the most difficult losses I would imagine that we as humans can experience is the loss of a child. Losing two daughters seemed like too much suffering for any one person. Sometimes, when I record one of these stories, I know I am meeting that person so we can help each other sustain our strength so that we might continue to care for other souls while also strengthening our own vibration of love.

A few days later on New Year's Eve, I was at a friend's house for the evening. Her friend Helena, whom I had never met before, sat down next to me. She revealed that she had been married to a rabbi and had later divorced. Her son, who was a doctor, was diagnosed with cancer and told he had one year to live at age 32. He had wanted to be a doctor from the time he was very young. He did live for seven years after that initial diagnosis and was able to practice and help many people. I remarked to Helena that in the stories I was relating in this book, I had met two other mothers who had lost their sons, both of whom were also young doctors, and I felt so sad that someone who studied long and hard, and who had great abilities and the empathy to care for others, didn't have much time to share their gifts. I also mentioned that I was aware that our lives are not measured by how long we have lived, but how much our soul has expanded in the way of feeling, and expressing love and compassion. Helena was much in tune with this thinking and discussion, and though she had suffered the physical loss of her husband, her son, and then her parents, she was still a vital and strong soul. She accepted her life and her challenges and I believe had a great respect and love for life.

It is perfectly all right and desirable to ask for help
from those around us and also from Spirit.

❖

Dianne, another woman I met at the party, then told me that she had a friend Joanne who was dating a Jewish man. The family was very unpleasant and condescending towards her. She said to me, "Sheryl, I know you understand the Christ consciousness even though you were born into a Jewish family." I told her that I believed all religions emphasized loving yourself and others as Jesus and other enlightened beings had highly suggested, but people simply had difficulty assimilating and implementing that simple truth into their lives. They internally understood the words but couldn't put them into practice. Often the ego identification with physical aspects of life did not allow the truest feelings of compassion to be shared from their heart. Those family members who were being unkind to that young woman were sleepwalking through life and simply not awakened souls, and she could only help them grow by continuing to be kind to them even though they weren't able to do that for themselves or for her yet.

It would seem I was not merely recording stories of coincidences and synchronicities but was becoming aware of the Oneness of all creatures and life as part of Divine energy.

This divine spiritual awakening, and the feeling of real love without expectations or controls, is not what I experienced earlier in my life due to my incessant need to achieve, be perfect, and be in control.

CHAPTER 27
Mediums from Lily Dale

And I think we'll be able to prove scientifically that other talents such as intuitive, psychic, clairvoyant, and clairaudient are very real.
Shirley MacLaine

Years ago, on a vacation to Pebble Beach, California, one of the most beautiful, spiritual places in creation, in my estimation, a woman who worked at the hotel took me in a minivan to a new spa at an adjoining hotel. Her name was Mary. She had originally lived in New York but had come to this area to pursue her spiritual interests. I told her about my mom's passing and how she had sent messages of three doves, which she had promised to do if she arrived safely in a dimension beyond, and I had received the dove messages many times since her passing.

Telling Mary about the many coincidences, which were a constant in my life, as well as the way I had come to understand spiritual energy as being tangible and real, I hoped Mary realized that souls visited us to help us both to continue their own development as well as ours. I relayed to Mary that as coincidences happened more frequently, a person's psychic energy was able to affect, restructure, and change their physical environment. When your soul energy is in tune with your physical energy, there is a process of manifestation from a higher consciousness of soul. The person's soul first needs to evolve to a vibration that rejects fear and darkness, and then manifesting or creating constant synchronicity and fulfilling goals of the soul begin to happen often. By the time a person is aware of this interactive divine intervention, they probably would also have developed great awareness of their intuitive and psychic abilities.

Mary dropped me off at the spa, which turned out to be a perfect, physically pleasing environment. Soon another coincidence transpired. The man who gave me my therapeutic body wrap was named Timothy, and he immediately told me he was not supposed to be working that day and had been assigned to me at the last minute. I quickly and breathlessly related stories of other Timothy's who had constantly appeared and been part of my dealing with painful experiences. The Timothy's I met in the past were sensitive and either in tune with religious understandings or involved in some way in a search into the nature of energy, miracles, and love, or simply interested in fun and adventure in their own lives. To me, they appeared divinely placed in my path at the right time. Spiritually advanced helpers may present as earth angels or living guides as the needs and interest of a person unfold.

Timothy was also working on an investigation of the origins of the Universe and was writing a book. We were both amazed at our less-than-random meeting, which enabled us to reinforce similar concepts and our awareness of the universality of all life forms. Before I left, he asked me to check out Zecharia Sitchin, a Russian-born American author whose books proposed an explanation for human origins involving ancient astronauts.

Mary picked me up from the spa at the appointed time, and upon returning to the hotel, she turned to face me and said, "You should visit Lily Dale, a small town on the border of Pennsylvania and New York, where spiritualism originated over 120 years ago. Nearly all the townspeople were psychic mediums with different talents and specialties. Classes were offered, and lecturers from all over came to share their knowledge and provide opportunities for people seeking a heightening of their own intuitiveness for energy readings and healing."

Months later, I attempted to make a trip to Lily Dale, which was quite a distance from my home. My work schedule made that trip impossible, and now a couple of years later, a group of practicing mediums from Lily Dale were in New York City. The Learning Annex sponsored a seminar. I had not gotten to Lily Dale; Lily Dale had come to me.

The day arrived, and I was off for the workshop, which included the mediums from Lily Dale. Each of the five mediums was incredibly gifted, well-trained, and most respectable looking. Many people seem to think that people developing these metaphysical abilities are off-beat, perhaps, strange, and maybe odd-looking. Many of the psychics whom I have met are attractive, well-educated, and involved in many professional areas of study and work. Years ago, I myself might have thought that people involved in these related mystical studies were way-out, but I am happy to say I was very wrong. After meeting such talented and gifted people from many different parts of the world who follow the path of mysticism, I have learned to respect and love the differences in people. This understanding has freed me of many of my earlier prejudicial beliefs, and I consider myself blessed and fortunate to be in a position of receptivity, to learn about dimensions beyond this world, and the interaction of energy sources throughout the Universe. Rather than just living in one environment, I function in two: the world of life and the world of Spirit. The possibility for enjoying life and communication between souls is like having an Internet within my mind and heart without the computer.

At the conclusion of the workshop, Rev. John White told the audience he had time for several private readings. I rushed outside, hoping to be one of the first in line, but to my extreme disappointment saw at least 15 people in front of me. Not thinking I had much of a shot for getting one of the coveted sessions, even though intuitively I sensed I was supposed to get a reading, I asked a girl wearing a nametag named Evelyn, if this was the right line to sign up for an appointment with John White. Evelyn asked my name, and I said, "Sheryl Glick." She ran over to the person taking down names and came back to me with a big smile as she told me my name was already on the list. Incredible, but then this group of mediums was probably one of the most elite working in the field. Their guides had already alerted them to those individuals who needed extra care, attention, and guidance.

The young woman went on to tell me I was fourth on the list, my appointment was at 7:30, and that it would be in room 2244. Those numbers are both master numbers, and I was excited beyond belief, knowing I was in for quite an interesting experience while also noticing the list with my name on it was computer-generated. At any rate, it was not handwritten, so I believed it was already prepared before the people had assembled and waited in line to try and get an appointment.

After a brief dinner in the hotel coffee shop, I proceeded to room 2244. John answered my knock on the door and invited me in. He sat down and told me to take off my coat and get comfortable. Then, he told me his eyes would be closed during the entire course of the reading and my voice vibration given when I said my name would help him. John began the reading by saying to me that my brain was being rewired for a more complete understanding of relationships and some of the nonsensical behavior of the past was no longer satisfying and wasted precious, life-sustaining energy. I thought perhaps he was suggesting that I no longer had to try so hard to get people to see the value of spiritual communication or that I did not need the acceptance or the acknowledgement from others who had different life paths to walk and who could not, at this time, accept the vision I have or the work that I do. Perhaps it meant I did not need to assume nor expect others to feel or act as I did or value what was important to me, as I was often disappointed when they didn't respond as I hoped.

Then John said that he saw a psychic line, not a physical line, in my hand in his inner vision, and it ran deep. There would certainly be an explosion of psychic-medium abilities. "Destiny," he said. "We're talking destiny here." Not being quick enough to ask the right question, I think I should have asked, "Where will this destiny take me?"

John then said. "You *had* a son."

"Yes, I *have* a son."

"He will be very prosperous and deal with millionaires. Say his name."

I responded, "Gregg William."

"Is there anything you want to ask me about your son?"

"He has type 1 diabetes," I said. "How is he handling this?"

John continued, "Gregg could control his disease with diet if he had a strong will or a medical patch to monitor it. Advancement in medical technology would be forthcoming."

Next, I asked about the book I was working on, and he said, "Do you have students yet?"

"Not exactly," I responded. I had several devoted Reiki clients with whom I discussed my understandings about energy and healing. He believed I would self-publish my first book and a student would help me. He also said it would be picked up by a publisher later, and he saw it in big print and felt in time, an Englishman would put up money to promote it. He believed it would be used for teaching and asked if it was a teaching manual. Then he said, "No, it is written more like a drama. There are other books to follow this one. They will be used as teaching tools."

John asked for my hand and shook it. He then said, "Now you have promised to teach Reiki."

I responded, "How can you make me promise to something before I even know what it is?"

"Spirit sometimes knows what we need before we know it ourselves. Let me tell you how you will begin your Reiki teaching. A teacher will leave, and you will have to teach the students."

At the time. I couldn't even imagine teaching a class. Reflecting on his message now, when I was ready to teach, I did ask my Reiki Master Teacher, Barbara, to help me with my first group of five students, and after that initial workshop, the students continued coming for training with me.

John White continued with further messages from Spirit and still held my hand, connected to my energy and aura, as he continued to say that my son would be prosperous, my daughter would do something without the help of a man, and my husband would be on television. Well, like all messages, they don't contain the whole story at that particular moment. So, I decided just to remember his words and wait to see what came next. Sometimes, it takes a while before prophecies or messages from Spirit are fulfilled. I often tuck them into the back of my mind, and when experiences happen, I am amused that it is so close to what was said to me previously.

Several weeks later, while coming home one evening, David rushed to the doorway to tell me he had been interviewed by a newscaster at the golf course and the segment would be airing on the seven-o'clock news. I had gotten home just in time to see David on television, and I remembered weeks before, I had been told by John White that this would indeed happen. Prophecies often come true if we are patient and trusting.

About a year later, my son, Gregg, called from California to tell me he had been selected by his company, an international insurance agency, to be included in a leadership group with several men from his company. The first meeting was in New York, and the next was in Ireland, the midpoint for several of the attendees. I was so proud to see Gregg so happy in his work and prospering just as John White had predicted.

In reflecting on the comment made by John White referring to my daughter achieving results without the help of a man, she was recently made vice president of a literary agency where she works with other women and was recently asked to participate in a conference at Rutgers University to evaluate and promote children's books. I was quite proud of her hard work and many achievements!

So much information to absorb, and now I finally understood why some people were afraid of receiving a reading from a medium. Often, they did not want to hear the truth or learn about a version of a reality different than what they desired. It was easier to live in a fantasy world, and while we all have introspective insights, we can discount them and hope and pray for what we believe we want.

Recently I had a client who was not happy with her reading, for I suggested she could not find the love she wanted, or felt she deserved, as she was filled with anger and pain and living with blame for others whom she believed had caused her unhappiness. She told me I was not telling her anything new, so it was the truth if she had been told this before. I suggested she find ways to improve her thoughts and activities that helped her let go of past hurts all the while finding more fun and joy in herself and therefore creating the person she could be and creating the life she wanted. She really only wanted a fortune teller to tell her she would get it all, but our future is determined by the choices and decisions we make, and the work we do in supporting our soul growth. Being consumed by physical needs will not support that possibility. Told long ago I was not a medium for everyone, I truly understand, through this person's discontent, that we cannot help or please everyone, as it is hard to find common ground with someone on a much different life path than with a person inspired by love and acceptance.

Therefore, I have learned it is not what we want, but what we need in order to accomplish our very reason for incarnating into this life. Eventually, reality and our life plan will come together and allow us to discover more about our deepest needs. Hopefully, they are one and the same and will match our destiny. We may at times have vague feelings about something that may happen that we are not yet ready to experience, so we might just push those feelings away. But our soul knowing will continue to offer experiences that prepare us to handle situations that, in the end, bring us a new understanding of ourselves and of life.

A Master Teacher, Caroline Myss

On Sunday, I proceeded to the Long Island Railroad train station to catch a train to the city to a lecture being offered by Caroline Myss, the author of *Anatomy of the Spirit: The Seven Stages of Power and Healing*. Ms. Myss is an accomplished medical intuitive, and I was hoping to hear her views. On the train, I sat across from two women. One was holding Caroline's new book, *Sacred Contracts*, and one of the ladies asked me if I was also going to the lecture. We seemed instantly connected by more than just our destination, and I soon discovered they were sisters named Rose and Anna. Rose was a psychologist and social worker, and Anna owned a hair salon in my hometown. Both were clearly knowledgeable about metaphysical matters, telling me about visitations in dreams they experienced, and were on their way to developing their psychic-medium abilities, as was I. Arriving at our destination, we entered the Manhattan Center and were amazed to see this large auditorium filled to the brim with so many people. Perhaps 1500 people or more were present. In the front area of the auditorium were tables loaded with books related to all holistic subjects. I selected several Reiki books, one on reflexology, and another on the art of forgiveness.

Why, I wondered, are so many more people at this event than at the lecture I had recently attended with the five psychics from Lily Dale? Caroline Myss began her lecture with a discussion of higher consciousness and her own story of how she had made a connection to God and developed her intuition as a result of new awareness.

❖

Caroline Myss was a funny, dynamic speaker. She jumped from thoughts in her first book to thoughts that she was expounding in her new book on inspirational acts and acts of loving kindness. She expressed that a physical way of relating to our world and our survival in a physical world, were based on instincts and those experiences related to the lower three chakras, or energy points, in our body. The four higher chakras helped us bypass time and space to reach higher levels of consciousness and assisted us in manifesting what our higher passions led us to value.

The question Caroline posed to the audience was, "Does one have the courage to manifest their vision for a better life? This vision would bring them past their financial fears, fears of being alone, or the fear of loss of control of their life as they knew it." As I thought about the client who had not responded well to being asked to accept responsibility for improving her life, this question showed me what she lacked to make the necessary changes: courage.

Obviously, many people would not be up for this challenge yet.

When one's perceptive skills allowed one to be introspective, there could be conflict between the "lowest" state of physical being and the "highest" state of the four higher chakras. Ms. Myss expressed that what we see and what we choose not to see relate to how well we could climb over the many fears that held us back from finding our true goals and desires.

Listening to Caroline Myss, I became aware that many of us who are working to achieve a higher state of consciousness seem to annoy or might inadvertently hurt people close to us, who might still be responding to life in the lowest survival mode. As we are able to respond more fully with love and peaceful actions, many others are not happy to see us moving towards enlightenment. They feel more insecure and are afraid of being left behind. However, souls reaching towards a state of higher being should not ask for permission to be extraordinary. It is becoming clearer to me when we refer to someone having an ordinary life rather than an extraordinary life that we are describing people who live contained in the needs, fears, and limits of their lower chakras as victims of the physical world. They have not yet encountered the extraordinary world of higher self that deals with the world of Spirit. To enter the realm of extraordinary life, where love, peace, contentment, and happiness reside, you must work to release the emotions of the lower chakras, including blame, jealousy, and other negative feelings, accepting everyone as extraordinary but knowing some are still functioning at a level of ordinary acceptance.

At this point in the lecture, there was a break. Upon returning to my seat, I realized I wasn't quite sure why I was at this seminar. I had been entertained up until now but hadn't heard any message of great personal importance. Then, at the very end of the session, Caroline told a story of a blind woman who lived at the time of the Revolutionary War. She was able to channel spirit. George Washington had come to her in Spirit and told her they had a book to write about his life. She told him she was blind, and he said for her to get someone to help her. She found a woman named Harriet Von Topol, and together they wrote the book for George Washington as he had intended. In the book, Washington mentioned Timothy's Tavern as a place where several of the Founding Fathers congregated. Later, when Caroline found this book and was able to get it published, she tried to find this mention of Timothy's Tavern but was unable to. Maybe the restaurant in Roslyn, New York, The George Washington Inn that Gloria and I had discussed and been to, was originally Timothy's Tavern. The owners had told us that Washington had indeed stopped there, and I remember being amused by the small door that led into the building. As I was listening to Caroline mention this fantastic story about a place George Washington visited long ago, I remembered I had dreamed of George Washington only recently and in that dream saw a little, dark, curly-haired girl sitting on a small stool with George Washington standing right in front of her.

Days later, while walking on the boardwalk near the ocean, I stopped for a moment, looked up, and saw a sign that read, "Washington Blvd." At that very moment, I realized that my son was Gregg William, G.W. Now here was an incredible story being told by Ms. Myss of George Washington. It seems the DNA of our ancestors and the DNA of humanity reside in our souls and resurface as needed. She went on to say that the Founding Fathers—Washington, Jefferson, Hancock, Adams and others at the Philadelphia courthouse—were told by a divine voice to proceed with the signing of the Constitution and the birth of this new nation under God. Mystical energy had always surrounded this country, and the Founding Fathers were also told by Spirit that they were members of a White Brotherhood of evolved souls, who had incarnated at that time in history to make this nation a powerful spiritual nation, an example for the entire world to emulate in the future.

Ms. Myss proceeded to inform the audience that we were headed for a global holistic theology and there would be a merging coalition of God's world and all religions at a deeper level. None of the existing religions would dominate, and they would all merge into one cooperative religion.

Humanity will heal their religious misconceptions and no longer be at odds. We will find the true purpose of all religions, which is Universal love and acceptance.

A few days after this conference, I entered the post office to purchase stamps. The woman behind the counter remarked to me that the stamps I was holding cost more than the normal package of 20 stamps. I asked which stamps she recommended. She held up a package of stamps with George Washington on them. It seemed appropriate for me to buy those stamps in honor of George Washington, our first president, a spiritual leader of evolved distinction who represented the goodness of our American Constitution and nation as the source for leadership in the world.

The challenges we are facing in our world and several important issues being brought into public view referencing the actions surrounding the recent presidential election of 2016 seem to be quite ubiquitous and distant from the will and needs of the people. Some interests by various groups show a lack of regard and respect for our beginning values by the Founding Fathers. Ours is a world that has imploded, where violence and lack of respect for ethics, lawfulness, and human life has been embraced by many people satisfied more with their physical needs being met and living ordinary instead of extraordinary lives. This has allowed an insensitivity to infect our thinking and behaviors as much as any disease of the physical body. Our politically correct leadership in search of global inclusiveness has lost a connectedness to the people's values, their bravery and courage, and the nation should not go forward without carrying our unique great traditions alongside modern-day world needs. Working to improve connections globally does not mean each country should have a loss of love for their history and uniqueness. Inclusiveness does not mean not honoring the past or cultural interests of other countries or ways they govern themselves. This craving to value our past achievements and any and all hardships need not diminish the special pride of any sovereign land. Nationalism is not a travesty. Therefore, the triumphs of the past will not be lost but honored and included as we move into the future.

Sometimes in the name of helping a specific cause or group, a person may show lack of concern for others, see only his own viewpoint, and damage his cause as well as our heritage. I am referring to what was recently seen when an NFL player refused to stand for the American Pledge of Allegiance. This country has allowed him and so many others opportunities he would not have had anywhere else on the planet. Instead of focusing on the failures he sees in the country in a hurtful, demeaning way, he could be a light of goodness in communities while working for the people he feels are oppressed.

Gratitude, forgiveness, and humility are the greatest virtues and precursors to real change.

CHAPTER 28
The Gift of a Medium

Each and every master, regardless of the era or the place, heard the
call and attained harmony with heaven and earth. There are many paths
leading to the top of Mount Fuji, but there is only one summit: Love.
Morihei Veshiba, Founder of Aikido

Driving along with me on a cold blustery winter night were several Reiki
students joining me to attend a demonstration of Afterlife Communication
being hosted by Robert Brown and James Van Praagh at the Hilton Hotel
in Melville. As a medium, I work individually on a one-to-one basis with
clients in a private setting while Brown and Van Praagh practice in front
of large audiences. Robert Brown has, over the years, encouraged me
to share messages this way, but I have found that no matter how many
mediums there are in the world, each one follows a plan for interacting
with the public that suits their soul needs and healing process.

Robert Brown and James Van Praagh are both sensitive mediums who
deliver messages in an upbeat and positive manner. There is an ethical
responsibility in giving messages. Messages must be given without judgment and personal interpretation, but exactly as received. The person
receiving the message can conclude what the images, words, songs, or
feelings mean without the spin by the messenger.

The event ended with a great round of applause for the presenters. My
students had greatly enjoyed the demonstrations of spiritual communication by these two famous psychic mediums. I quietly observed that most
of the readings were directed to parents who had lost young children.

After the event, the ladies and I made our way to the hotel restaurant.
We were seated at a large table, and there were very few patrons present.
I noticed a woman who had been seated in the row in front of me during
the demonstration approach our table. She asked the women how they

had liked the presentation. Then she turned to me and said, "Something about you has drawn me to meet you. I seem to need to speak with you."

"Perhaps you feel that energy because I am an energy practitioner and medium," I responded. She told me her mom had passed 15 years ago, but I sensed that was not why I had seen her crying during the demonstration. That was not the source of her obvious distress. I told her my mom had passed and that it helped me greatly to know that she survived physical death and was very much alive in a different dimension of eternal life.

She then blurted out, "My son died two months ago. He was 13. He was diagnosed with cancer when he was eight years old." I was startled by her revelation and felt the deep sadness of her loss intellectually and also intuitively in my heart. I hugged her, and I told her that perhaps her son's energy was around me. I worked with children, and children always flocked around me. I asked her name, which was Mary Beth, and her son had been Michael.

I took her address, as she lived out of state, and told her I would do a reading and promised to call her within a week's time. She had had a reading with Robert Brown that was comforting. Perhaps I would be shown something further that would help her and her family. My intention was to help this young woman who was directed, I believed, by Spirit to me.

I did call Mary Beth the next week as promised. While doing a reading for her at my office, I realized she had two other children who very much needed her to be well and to release the anger, pain, and sadness she still felt over the loss of her child. The reading brought tears of joy and release to both of us. My guides and Michael had outdone themselves and given Mary Beth the most fitting answers to her most challenging questions. In one of the messages I received, I sensed that her son had been in the bed in the middle of her husband and herself watching television. Michael had felt so safe and loved. Mary Beth began to cry. She said her son had passed in bed with them there. Michael was so grateful that he had such great parents. He also let his mom know that a grandparent met him and he was happy and safe. After the reading, Mary Beth told me she was aware that her son would continue to be involved with his family and knew she had to spend quality, loving time with her young daughters, who needed her to be joyful and happy and everyone had done their best during those difficult years and now needed to focus on the love shared, not dwell in the sadness.

Reaching out to others helps to bridge time, space, and distance so we may support, honor, and love each other, making divine connections.

❖

My spiritual messages do not exclusively or often portray future events of major consequence.

Several times in the past, I have received a sense of an impending death. Initially, I didn't make the connection between the message and the inevitability of a passing. That was perhaps a blessing, as I did not agonize over what could not be changed. Almost 31 ago, I walked into a cousin's bar mitzvah party and saw my joyful, smiling Aunt Gladys walking towards me. A thought flew by me: *She doesn't have long to live.* I was horrified, as I didn't know why I would think such a thing. Three years later, she died.

It was as a practicing healer and medium long after my aunt's passing that I experienced a similar feeling. During a session, I could feel my client wasn't eating and there was a sense of weakness in his lower body. He had collapsed in the shower that morning. During the healing session, I envisioned a tall, thin man of light at his solar plexus and remarked that he was a very beautiful, spiritual man. Knowing he was headed to his medical doctor after leaving me, I encouraged him to follow the plan of treatment that would be set up for him. It appeared to me he might be suffering from depression and might benefit from the right medication or treatment. I asked him to call me and let me know how he was doing. Three months later, upon hearing he had passed from someone in the neighborhood, I realized at the time of his Reiki session, I had picked up the future and that his energetic soul body would be departing. Upon reflection, I believe he may have known at the time of his visit to me what the message implied, but had just thanked me and then looked deep into my eyes with a kind, knowing expression of gratitude.

Life and death are in each of our soul's plan and will happen as designated by our destiny. There is nothing to fear, as life continues eternally in energy form.

❖

Caroline, one of the workers at the office, asked me if instead of getting the women holiday presents as I usually did, could we all go to a Broadway show? We had gone to a show the previous year and had an amazingly good time. Last year we had seen *Wicked*. The story was about how what we appear to see might actually be quite different from what is really happening. The bad witch in the show was not all bad, just as the good witch was not all good. This duality that lies within all of us allows us the opportunity to explore aspects of our emotions in order to find balance and harmony.

I told Caroline that might be a good idea. Before too long, I had eleven people scheduled to attend. I needed a show where the ticket prices would not break the bank. A day or two later, a card arrived at my home that advertised the first performances of *The Little Prince* in Lincoln Center. There were to be only eight performances. I asked if the group would like to experience this ballet and then proceeded to get tickets for all of us. Synchronicity was happening once again in a delightful manner. On a trip to Dubrovnik, Croatia, in a small gift shop, I was handed the well-loved French children's book *The Little Prince* by the young woman behind the counter. Having only a few coins in Croatian money left, I had just enough money to purchase this book.

In the story, a prince from a faraway galaxy cared for a small single rose. Feeling restricted in his small world, the young prince felt he needed to travel near and far to learn more about life. On his extended journey, he met some interesting characters while becoming aware at the very same time that no matter where he went, he continually thought about the beautiful rose he had nurtured and cared for on his small planet. Finally, he concluded that he needed to be with that one rose he had nurtured, as all his experiences were empty without love, and in essence, that rose was love and was the only lasting reality for him.

The trip and the performance at Lincoln Center were extraordinary, and we had a very interesting excursion. Bringing people of different sensibilities together quite spectacularly in feelings of goodwill and joy to be connected in love and good times—rather than focusing on the bad or unpleasantness in each of us—is the prime key to true lasting success.

CHAPTER 29
The Need for Different Levels of Healing

Be strong and courageous. Do not be terrified, do not be discouraged,
for the Lord your God will be with you wherever you go.
Joshua 1:9

I was invited to attend a concert for one of my clients Mike, who was twelve years old. The concert was for an organization collecting funds to support research for autism. As I didn't have a gift for Mike, I stopped at a local florist and selected a beautiful bouquet of flowers for him. While waiting for the florist to wrap them, I noticed a tiny porcelain box with a miniature lion, zebra, giraffe, and elephant. It was very inexpensive, and since I love collectible boxes, I purchased it. I hurried to the temple and was pleasantly surprised to enjoy a fantastic concert by a popular Israeli performer. Her voice was most beautiful, and the words of her songs were filled with spiritual sentiments of a pure and higher consciousness. It was so peaceful and also full of the joy of life.

At the end of the concert, Mike's mother, Barbara, presented me with an exquisitely wrapped present. Barbara is so generous and open-hearted and has been one of my most devoted Reiki students for years. Now, when a present is given to me, I receive it graciously and never refuse, as it is always an expression of love and it is in the giving and receiving that hearts connect.

I took the small package and told her I would open it on Chanukah. However, my curiosity overcame me once I was home, and I decided to peek in the box. Sometimes, we are all just small, curious children, unable to wait for the surprise. When I tore off the paper my eyes grew wide with surprise. I saw a beautiful, blue enamel statuette replica of what I had purchased for myself earlier: the same four animals; the animals on both were even in the same order or position.

However, on this trinket, there was one additional animal, a deer, and I was acutely reminded of a spiritual teacher who had told me long ago that he saw that forest animal representative of my energy and sensitivities. He had remarked that this was the only animal that cried when shot through the heart and was the most sensitive spiritual animal, much like a medium that feels the sting of another's pain. Recently, I had met a healer who took one look at my face and told me that my heart was my greatest asset and my greatest weakness. I have noticed when I receive painful messages from Spirit for my clients, I can feel the pain reflected in my own body for a short time. This sensation helps me to pinpoint the issues, whether of body or mind, that the client is dealing with. It seems also to help them talk through and release any negative perceptions that have created the pain or dysfunction in the first place.

> *It is in the letting go of that which no longer*
> *serves us that we are truly free.*

❖

I have not had a message specifically from my mom in a while, although I often feel shifts in energy around me and am grateful to know she and other helpful souls are touching base with me. I can at times feel the coolness passing over my shoulders or face, and at that moment, I know I am not alone. It is comforting. I felt that shift of energy around me today.

When I arrived at work, I found out that Kathie, who is the mother of four children, had just lost her father. Kathie was extremely devoted to Edward, her father. Kathie told me that before she was born, her father knew he would have another child and was expecting her even though her mother was not. He further knew what she would look like and explained in detail how excited he was about this special child, whom he named Jelly Bean in his dreams.

Indeed, her mother became pregnant, and Kathie was born, and when he saw her, he said, "That's the baby I dreamed of." Recently her father had been ill, but his passing came unexpectedly in a poignant and beautiful way. He was in bed with his wife and told her, "I love you," and then quietly passed. Kathie told me at the wake that the day before her father passed, they had gone to the beach and shared some special, joyful moments together. Only a few days prior to his passing, I had innocently asked Kathie how her parents were doing. For Kathie, the loss of her father was extremely hard. All the family members knew that this girl, Kathie, a late-in-life child, was a joy to him and that father and daughter shared a unique spiritual bond.

Our soul understands bonds of love and awareness of events even before the actual physical manifestations.

❖

We often do not have enough time to take care of certain everyday issues, but it is important to try to find time to support a soul mate if you are permitted to. Of course, everyone we interact with is a soul mate. Every person we interact with offers the opportunity to experience new emotions and feelings, ultimately guiding us to know more about our own being and theirs. I believe in the life plan we established before being born; each soul promised to interact with others in ways that could afford physical and spiritual awareness and growth. Soul mates are not necessarily love objects in the romantic sense, but beings of love in the universal merging of life energies for unity and oneness.

Often Spirit's message is very subtle and can be missed if one is not paying attention.

❖

On my way to the Bahamas for a workshop on healing energy, I met up with Pam and Sue, two of Robert Brown's assistants, in the LaGuardia Airport. While we waited for the plane, I was happy to give Pam a reading that I had done for her at my office prior to the trip. She was terribly nervous about flying, which I had not been aware of until I did her reading.

I didn't know too much about her personal life, though I found her to be a lovely, efficient, positive person whenever I had interactions with her. The first message in my reading addressed her anxiety and fear about flying, and the last message referred to a tripod landing softly on the moon. One must know how delicate a maneuver the craft must perform to accomplish that kind of touchdown.

The landing in the Bahamas was a dream, soft and perfect, and so the reading suggested to Pam that she had nothing to worry about on this flight.

Beautiful messages from Spirit to begin the trip and a beautiful happening to end it.

On the last day of the workshop, twelve people from the group met for lunch. I sat in the middle of four tables that had been put together. I usually opt for an outside seat so I don't feel constricted. One of the women with whom I had not spent much time during the workshop sat down next to me. She mentioned she had recently lost her husband, who had been ill with face and throat cancer for eight years and had many reconstructive surgeries, but the cancer kept returning. It had been a long and arduous battle that could not be won. I could only feel tremendous compassion for their suffering.

My hands and body began to feel very hot, and I mentioned this to Betty. She then said that she had cancer and had been operated on for stomach tumors. It seemed the Universe wanted me to use Reiki on her. I asked if she would want me to try Reiki on her, and she said she did. I felt tingling and some pain at her solar plexus. She said my hand was right over the exact spot of the incision. When the tingling subsided, I knew I had done all I could and hoped that she would find a practitioner in her area for continued therapy.

Relationships are mirrors of ourselves. What we attract always mirrors either qualities we have or beliefs we have about our relationships.
Louise L. Hay

Most teachers who see even the tiniest spark of enthusiasm and, indeed, love for learning that a student might display for the work being taught is delighted. Such was the joy I recently experienced when six of my students insisted, we attend workshops being offered at Lily Dale, New York. Lily Dale, located near Buffalo, New York, has been a growing community of people for the last 150 years who are spiritualists, healers, psychic mediums, and metaphysical scientists who have chosen to work together during the summer months. Many noted people in the field offer workshops there.

Three years ago, I attended a workshop in New York City featuring five spiritual teachers from Lily Dale and was aware of their highly developed abilities and that they helped other developing healers and mediums. Being with such powerful healers or mediums seemed to heighten other people's awareness and even their abilities. At that time, I received a reading from Rev. John White, a resident medium, who told me I would have help with the book I must write. Here, only three years later, I was at Lily Dale standing right in front of him with my students next to me as I handed him a copy of my book *Life Is No Coincidence: The Life and Afterlife Connection.*

The area was fresh and alive with grassy hills, valleys, sunshine, and farms spread out into the distance. The trees seemed greener and the air cleaner than in some other places I have been. As we drove from our hotel to Lily Dale for a night class, I noticed the moon was bright and alive with possibilities. As we followed John White's meditation, relaxing into the vibration of his voice and the music, I felt the energy to be just as he described before starting the meditation, noticing subtle changes taking place in the room. I believe the vibration of like-minded souls gathering for the purpose of their own personal growth is stronger collectively. People actually felt more alive and healthier when in such a conglomerate of positive thought and energy.

❖

I have noticed over time that clients don't always come into the office for their scheduled appointment. Sometimes they miss their appointment and reschedule. Sometimes they do not come at all. Perhaps Spirit has a change of plan for us. Whether it's a week or three weeks later, when my client does come in and we review the intuitive reading I have done prior to the scheduled meeting, the messages from Spirit are always appropriate and timely.

For example, on one occasion I sensed a headache developing on the left side of my forehead at the time prior to the session. The client responded to me that the headache just began while on the drive to the office that day, but I had done this reading three weeks previous to the session. I feel the guides or loved ones who are giving this information to me know exactly what day my client will arrive and adjust their information to accommodate the other person's time schedule. Mediums or psychics often see the future, past, and present merged together, for all events might be happening simultaneously on different planes of existence. It also seems that people who come for sessions are actually guided to the right practitioner at the right time.

❖

Recognizing that you are but one part of the total healing experience does not require that you attain some Zenlike state of detachment.
Eric Pearl, D.C.

New Healing Systems

I was so impressed with the intensity of the energy force I felt at Ruth Rendely's first class at the Learning Annex in New York that I made the decision to go to San Francisco to take an additional course with her. If the class had been somewhere other than San Francisco, this might not have happened, but my son is in San Francisco, and I would be able to visit him as well as take the class. One of my students, Karen, now also a Reiki Master and truly committed to her own personal growth and the healing of others, accompanied me.

She had booked her flights by herself and had a stopover in Salt Lake City, Utah, for the return flight. My flight home was straight through. I suggested that she might change her flight so we could go home together.

As airline rates are constantly changing, if she did it immediately, she might get a good rate. She decided to wait to change her ticket until later.

Several days later, we were off to California and had a very pleasant flight. We arrived at the Marriott Hotel on Fisherman's Wharf, checked in, and quickly headed to lunch at one of my favorite places, Johnny Rockets. Then, we took a cable-car tour of the city. We walked on Pier 39, a scenic tourist and shopping area, crowded with people visiting from many locales. We were able to absorb a great deal of the flavor of the area in a short time. I have been to California many times, but this was Karen's first trip, and I wanted her to experience as much of this fantastic city as possible before we began classes.

The next morning, we made our way to Union Square, the heart and hub of San Francisco. It was early and quiet. We arrived at the King George Hotel, a small, boutique, English-style setting where the workshop was to be held. I have found that all the events I attend for my continued growth are hosted and presented in tasteful and appealing locations. It might be that many spiritually minded individuals are older souls who may have shared lifetimes as well as experiences exposing them to areas surrounded by beauty of design, sound, and expression.

The room was already filling with participants. I was surprised and delighted to see there were actually more men in this group than women. Most people assume spirituality is more suited for the feminine gender. However, since all human beings have both male and female energy, we need to understand and develop these dual, energetic, unique sources within us. It is necessary for everyone to realize that spirituality or self-growth is a positive force for every man, woman, and child.

Karen and I started a discussion with two men who were seated directly behind us. One was a physicist from Canada, and the other was a biochemist from Greece. It seems there are people who can merge spirituality with scientific knowledge. The understanding of life and who we are, in my opinion, can only be approached from attention to both ends of the spectrum. Neither spirituality nor science can be the winner. Spirituality and science must be equal participants in an ongoing revelation and exploration of life, death, and the realms beyond this physical earth plane.

The man from Greece was named George, and he said he hoped to open a Center for Alternative Medicine when he returned to Greece. I told him that one of the offices I worked in was such a center. All types of energy healing were available, which included chiropractic, acupuncture, Reiki, massage therapy, homeopathic nutritional counseling, occupational therapy, and physical therapy.

Sitting directly to my right was a man who was a teacher working with teenagers with addictions. He told me he had studied in the Yucatán and while there, visited an ancient pyramid where he had learned techniques passed down from the healers and their ancient traditions. He also told me after one of the meditations he engaged in while in a Yucatan pyramid, he had a vision seeing himself swimming in the water towards a modern city, and he thought it was the ancient city of Atlantis.

"How strange that you tell me that story," I said. While doing our meditation this morning, I sensed I was underwater and swimming towards a magical island with tall glass buildings trimmed with golden, geometric-shaped borders. I seemed to be breathing underwater and moving quite quickly, although I had no breathing apparatus attached to me. It appears it was indeed my soul body having an out-of-body experience. "Was I swimming towards Atlantis in a time long ago, as you did?"

All the people in this workshop appeared to be seasoned metaphysicians involved in many diverse areas of study and New Age therapies. Toward the end of the workshop, Ms. Rendely wanted to share a meditation, utilizing and helping us to absorb certain energies from what she called the Venusian aspect, as she also taught classes on planetary influences. We do take on energies from others around us, so it is not a far stretch to think we might also take on interplanetary influences. This was a new awareness for me, but I have learned there is merit to many unique and different old-time ways to know more about our human and divine predilections.

Not long ago, I studied a psychological system involving human body types in a book called *Human Types Essence and the Enneagram*, by Susan Zannos, which expresses an idea that there are basically seven body types. Each body type exhibits certain personality traits and predispositions common to that particular body type. Certain body types are more in alignment with specific matches and feel more comfortable with those people and their energies. Once we understand people can only respond a certain way according to their personality, which is greatly affected by their body type, it may be easier to accept behavior that might seem to be misunderstood or unpleasant to us, as basically that is the most natural way for that person to respond to the environment. Not taking too much notice or being critical of questionable behavior or actions so different from our own can help us maintain balance in every situation.

After those thoughts, I put my full attention back to Ms. Rendely as she suggested the Venusian energy that would wash over us as a result of this mediation would be strong for the next few weeks and we might experience loving and pleasant events. It sounded nice to me, even if it was a little way out there.

When we left the class, it was raining. I had not brought my umbrella. Suddenly an older man stopped at my right side and told me we could get a taxi by the hotel a block away. He had a very large umbrella and held it over us as we walked. I noticed the man had a limp and walked slowly, and it was hard to walk that slowly in the pouring rain. He remarked that he was from New Orleans and had lived in New Jersey at some point. He asked if I liked Frank Sinatra's songs, and I said, "Of course I do." I wasn't sure what made him ask me that or why I responded the way I did. Perhaps I liked the otherworldly quality and tone of Frank Sinatra's voice and his mellow songs. When we got closer to the hotel, I thanked the man and then bounded quickly forward to get into a cab with Karen. I was grateful for his kind help. Perhaps a little bit of that Venusian wash of love that Ruth Rendely had promised was really happening.

We rushed to our hotel to freshen up and then took a cab to meet Gregg and Lea, his girlfriend, at an Italian restaurant. The food and service were spectacular even though we had a long wait. I was speaking to a man from Los Angeles who was a cameraman. There was a mother and little girl from New Jersey. I wondered if she liked Sinatra's music. I never did ask her.

❖

Earlier at our hotel in trying to resolve a problem with Karen's flight home to New York, Karen had called the airline to change her ticket so we could travel home on a nonstop flight together. The airline wanted an additional 550 dollars, and there was no way that Karen would pay that. It appeared we would both have to go on different flights. Neither of us was thrilled about this prospect.

The next day when we arrived at the airport, I checked my bag outside, but Karen said she would hold hers since she had a stopover flight. The man gave me my boarding ticket and sent us inside so Karen could get her ticket. I suggested we wait on the service line and try again to get the ticket changed. When we got to the ticket counter, a girl with dark, beautiful hair, sea-foam eyes, and a friendly smile was there to help us. There was no line, and this was encouraging. We told her that Karen wanted to change her flight to be on my nonstop flight to New York.

"Could we change it?" I asked.

Well, she said, "You're lucky. I have one seat left in first class, and it is discounted." I thought it would probably be too much money, even discounted. "Wait," the receptionist said, "I see that Karen has already been rerouted to your flight because of weather conditions in Salt Lake City. Here's your ticket, and there is no additional charge."

Karen and I looked at each other and screamed, "Wow, Venusian love was really happening." When we got to our gate and sat down, I went to shut off my cell phone and noticed I had a message from Cory, the young man we had been talking about last evening. When I told Karen, she said, "No way, that's too weird."

"Why is it any weirder than your tickets being changed before we asked for the change?" We were laughing, and whether it was magic or not, intentions were honored by the Universe because we had asked for it, and it was a delightful expression of things working out well. Whether it was the law of attraction, positive thoughts, or just love rewarding us for continued hard work and service to others, Karen and I enjoyed the fun.

❖

On Mother's Day, I spoke to Gregg and was giving him a reading while he and Lea were driving in the car. I don't often do readings for my family members unless there is a specific need or I am asked to. It seemed Spirit knew I would be talking to him while they were in the car that day, as an event I had sensed a week ago would be unfolding while they were driving.

Gregg said that Lea made a giant bowl of pasta and salad on Sunday just as I had envisioned while doing his reading. I then told Gregg another message I had sensed of a feeling of some kind of gentle motoring on a curvy road, and there was such an open, beautiful view. The activity and ride felt like a lot of fun. Most of the men I give readings to often don't want to discuss the meaning of the impression. I believe they need more time to assimilate the information and process it. They are also somewhat more cautious and reserved with their emotional responses. Gregg just grunted when I read this message. I spoke to Lea for a few minutes. Gregg abruptly asked for the phone back and said to me he had just seen a sign that said, "Winding Road Next 8 Miles."

"Am I going to have an accident?" he asked.

"No, of course not. Just go gently and enjoy the view and the ride."

Spirit knew I would be talking to Gregg at the time this driving event was unfolding. It was dramatic and might leave a strong imprint on Gregg or Lea. I feel he as well as his sister and my grandchildren are intuitively gifted, as so many of us are, and are already using this awareness in many positive ways professionally and personally, even though not totally aware they are doing this.

CHAPTER 30
Each of Us Receives Whispers from Spirit

Let us not become weary in doing good, for at the proper
time we will reap a harvest if we do not give up.
Galatians 6:9

I am off to visit a person who is very ill and try, as always, to hold onto my strong sense of faith even in what appear to be dismal circumstances. At times, I struggle to have trust in each person's life plan, especially those lives so different from my own, and must try even harder to conquer feelings of judgment. Knowing that each person's values, beliefs, and the uniqueness of individualized experiences and situations are there to both witness and benefit from so we may learn acceptance is still a challenge at times.

I have also tried to overcome fear of disease and death. Since there is no death, only a changing of our energetic, physical structure to another form of existence and energy, I feel it may be possible to help others who struggle to understand the fragility of the human condition.

If I can, and when guided by Spirit, I hope to help others
cross over and pass with dignity and less resistance.

At hospice, I was directed to a young man only 44 years old. His name was Shawn. In quick order, he told me he was dying and couldn't wait to go home. His life had been difficult, and he was spiritually aware of the concept of reincarnation. He felt life and death were part of the continuing evolution of our soul. Shawn showed me several worn and well-read books about Edgar Cayce, who was a prophet and medium. Somehow Shawn knew I was a hands-on energy healer and medium and asked if I could give him a reading. I told him I would close my eyes and see what happened. Shawn was very happy to hear that spiritual loved ones surrounded him. I sensed he had shown much love and done so with an open heart and told him he lived by the water and had a niece with big eyes whom he cared greatly for. He had been to Florida as a boy and seen palm trees for the first time. He acknowledged all these statements to be true.

I sensed that Shawn was much like the Biblical character David in the story of David and Goliath. With a slingshot, Shawn had tried to fight injustice. He was a man with an open heart and love, despite his difficult childhood. I mentioned some of the challenges that I had dealing with people who were not able to understand my spiritual work. Shawn told me to treat those people with extra goodwill and joyfulness, as it would throw them off, and they wouldn't be able to disturb me. It seemed like good advice, and then Shawn said, "Avoid such people, as your path leads into light and healing. Like finds like, and if you feel uncomfortable when someone enters your energy field, remove yourself."

I wished Shawn good luck and peace and asked him not to talk about this reading with the staff, as it was not part of the requirements of my duties. As I went over to the front desk to sign out for the day, I saw one of the bereavement counselors, Sister Catherine, approach me. She told me there was a young man who had asked to see a medium, as he wanted to determine if he had used his time while here on earth wisely. She asked if I was a medium. "Yes, I am," I told her. She and I went in to see Shawn together.

We both went in to talk to him. He was hesitant to tell Sister Catherine anything we had discussed. Then Sister Catherine told him that God had answered his recent request and provided a medium and it wasn't a coincidence.

"Well," he responded, "synchronicity has happened to me over the course of my entire life, and I am not surprised." Sister Catherine has always been quite supportive of my efforts at helping patients and was aware that the love and kindness that God sends through a medium at appropriate times can help in many ways. Help can come from a layperson as well as from a theologian.

There are no special labels or credentials needed for one to be a conduit for God's message of love, for often the words and glances of human beings to one another are influenced and guided by Spirit, as we are all the bearers of light, wisdom, kindness, and truth, even when unaware of this wondrous influence.

❖

Mother's Day was approaching!

When I returned home that evening, I received an e-mail from Dr. Judith Orloff, whom I had met at Lily Dale months before. She was presenting an awareness workshop in Phoenix, Arizona, the next weekend, and remote viewing as an energy process was going to be discussed. I thought I might already be using a remote-viewing technique to receive messages but really wasn't sure. I found out that remote viewing is a form of meditatively looking at a subject and gathering information, impressions, and psychic awareness to help discover more about the subject in question. I was curious to learn more.

I asked David if he would like to give me this trip as my Mother's Day gift. Of course, he did. He does not actively subscribe to my beliefs of energy healing and afterlife, but he does encourage the leeway I need to spiritually advance. In that way, he is the most special of husbands, as to allow a partner to develop and advance according to their own standards and life plan which is necessary for the health and wellbeing of all.

Intrigued by the concept of remote viewing, I thought Dr. Stephen Schwartz, who would be discussing the subject, was someone I had met at Robert Brown's retreat last spring. So, I made the final decision to attend this conference. However, when I arrived in Phoenix for the conference, I found that this was not the case. The man I met in the Bahamas last year was Dr. *Gary* Schwartz. Here I was off to Arizona for this event under a mistaken pretense, but it didn't matter! Whatever or however I had chosen to go, it would be the absolute right experience for me. Many presenters at this conference were active and prominent in the fields of music and art for therapeutic and spiritual value.

While in Phoenix, I met a young woman from England. Her professional name was Bliss, but her real name was Lucinda. When she walked out on the stage and I heard the vibration and sound of her voice, I felt a resounding burst of understanding of deep heart truths reflected in the beauty of the words she sang. I could feel her commitment and connection both to Spirit and humanity. It was like a mirror to my own being, and the sadness and joy of her music were confirmations of my own personal destiny. Her song moved my soul, and I actually cried. Later I found out she had studied for twelve years with Indian gurus.

Later the same day, Bliss and her back-up musician, Marcus, ran into me, and we spent some time together. Bliss remarked that she observed within me great "personal power." I gave her a copy of my book and remarked that I felt I had many personal connections to England and its history. She would find that apparent as she read the book. I purchased Lucinda's musical CD and brought it back to New York to share with my clients, deeply aware that her music and that of others at the event provided a sense of deep inner harmony and quietness inspired by guides in Spirit, and I was very grateful that I had experienced the beauty of their music.

At the same time, I had a reading by a palm reader. Her daughter was also clairvoyant. She told me to have a colonoscopy, as I might have a polyp. It was not a problem but needed to be removed, and indeed I did, and a polyp was removed. I was, at some point, also to check my carotid artery, as there could be a blockage due to hereditary influences, and I have also done that, but at this time, there is no issue. However, the good news was I would live a long life. Eventually, within five years, I would be traveling and signing my books.

I was to get started on my new book. According to this medium, I had already been given the idea about eight months ago, and I was to relay in this book how Spirit whispers with love and guidance to help us complete our life plan. She also told me music was very important to me, and there would be a love for life and more intimate, higher levels of love in all my relationships.

She went on to tell me I was an author, healer, and teacher and had two sons. One son came in and went away, and the other son—a son not by birth but a son nevertheless—stayed close by. She said I had had a difficult childhood as an indigo child but had asked to do more with my intuitive ability and was now functioning as a crystal being. Crystal beings are those with divine purpose and light to bring real changes. Like the main character in the film *It's a Wonderful Life*, I couldn't see the wide scope of all I was doing. Then her daughter, also an intuitive, offhandedly told me to write my next book and not wait till I was 81 years old. The readings seemed to be a validation of certain events that I had already experienced. Other events, I knew, would ultimately unfold.

Years later when I was the host of a global network radio show on the internet, I reached out to Lucinda Bliss Drayton, and she was one of the first guests on my show, *Healing From Within*. The seeds for the future were sown at that meeting years before, and I had briefly questioned why I had even gone, as I sometimes do. In reality, we all are where we are meant to be, driven by either soul, need, purpose, or guides in Spirit.

❖

Sitting at my desk waiting for my client to come, I thought about a woman whom I had met in Arizona. Her name was Victoria. She was seated next to me in a music sound bowl healing workshop I attended while at the conference. I initially noticed she was more attractive and quieter or calmer in nature than many of the other participants. It was only a fleeting observation. Later, I got to see her display table, where Victoria had a DVD displayed showing unusual orbs and light objects on the cover. She also had a musical CD with angelic tones for healing. As she spoke to me, I noticed her voice was melodious and delightful.

Victoria told me she had been encountering guidance from extraterrestrials since she was a child. I asked if she found them to be friendly and what they looked like. Yes, they were friendly, and they looked like her: blonde, quiet, and calm. They were here, as was she, to help humanity.

Thinking about it, aren't we all ETs? Our spirit and soul come from a higher plane of energy, or star dust, and combine with a physical body. Some light workers are here to improve the human condition. Others are here mainly for earthly or physical experience, but we are all Spirit. I might have been slightly judgmental when listening to Victoria describe she was connecting to extraterrestrial light beings. Was it so out of the ordinary? Years ago, I would have totally freaked out at such an announcement, but since I know all is illusion in this physical world, I cannot say one way or the other whether there is truth or falseness in this woman's claim.

However, Victoria was a lovely woman who never had her own children but had helped raise her husband's five children. She told me her story had been acquired by director Ron Howard and would be made into a mainstream movie. I did so enjoy listening to her healing music and shared the music with my students. While sharing this story now, years after the event, I realize I recently interviewed Hollywood actress Dee Wallace, author of *Bright Light*, about her spiritual insights and beliefs. She portrayed the mother in the feature film E.T. *The Extra-Terrestrial*. Was this coincidence, fate, or divine intervention? Looking back from my vantage point now and having opened up to realms of intelligence and wisdom from higher dimensions that assist me in my personal development and help me to refine my innate spiritual talents, I realize that over the last few years, I have interviewed a group of scientists exploring infinite possibilities for life beyond what we can know in this three-dimensional world and have been amazed to listen to extraterrestrial stories in a more open-minded fashion. I have interviewed many notable guests who are exploring the extraterrestrial phenomenon. Robert Salas, author of *Unidentified: The UFO Phenomenon* and a graduate of the USAF Academy with a degree in Aerospace Engineering, now retired from the Air Force, offers extensive testimony and documentation by military officers and airmen of their eyewitness accounts of UFO occurrences, alien abductions, and threats to military installation. Another guest on my internet radio show, *Healing From Within*, was Betty Andreasson, a warm and everyday kind of individual who was studied extensively by government agencies for her remarkable drawings and descriptions of her 1967 abduction by what she described as entities who made her feel they were friendly and peaceful. Still another wonderful guest was Ted Peters, author of *UFOs: God's Chariots?*, who has spent a lifetime exploring the many events and reports worldwide by people who have experienced interactions with higher beings. Most recently, I have interviewed Nancy Du Tertre, author of *How to Talk to an Alien*. As the other guests, her credentials and credibility are impeccable.

Again, I think how happy I am that I am now finally open to ideas that years ago were foreign and hostile to me. How I wish more people would listen to their own instinctive wisdom and, without judgment, allow what comes next, as life builds and creates even greater life possibilities. However, many people still resist hearing or seeing something completely new or different than their expectations and as a result, denounce or fear what is unknown. The possibilities for creating new relationships with the world, Universe, and its evolving people make for such great fun and creative expression.

❖

After returning from Arizona, I went into one of my favorite eateries near my office. Sitting there right in front of me was Steven Engel, my boss from several years ago. It is interesting how the Universe or our Spirit guides bring us together with people to share messages and encourage us to fulfill our destiny. I am always so happy when I run into Steven or his father, Philip Engel. They are two dynamic, enthusiastic, energetic people, and I worked with them for ten years in a very successful furniture business. Steven was with his 13-year-old daughter, and she had grown so pretty. I could see how proud Steven was of her.

"Well," said Steven, "I so enjoy looking at your book *Life is No Coincidence*. I especially liked the stories that took place in California." For the moment, I couldn't even remember those stories. It has been some time since I have looked at my own book. Like everything else in our lives, once it is over, it almost seems like it was a dream. For me, there is no reason to relive it again, as new adventures and experiences present themselves regularly.

"Steven, I am told by other mediums and psychics that I have to begin my next book, but since the first one was not a blockbuster, does it make sense to do another book?"

Steven responded, "I don't know about authors, but music is where I put most of my attention. I know a songwriter. His first CD was not much. He produced a second, and that was also not the success he had hoped for, but on the third try, he hit it big. His name was Bruce Springsteen." How wondrous that Steven was so delightfully encouraging and so enthusiastic about my work. He seemed almost like an earth angel bringing to me higher words of wisdom.

I met Steven again several years down the road at a wake for my colleague Roseanne's husband. Roseanne's son was dating Steven's niece, and other than that connection, it is probable that Steven might not have been there that night. It gave me pleasure to see him and remind him that his words of encouragement had some part in my finishing my second book, *The Living Spirit: Answers for Healing and Infinite Love*, and now you are reading the third book in the trilogy, *A New Life Awaits: Spirit Guided Insights to Support Global Awakening*.

On Monday night, I went to a workshop concentrating on the topic of remote viewing and out-of-body experiences. Remote viewing was explained in much the same way as at the recent convention in Arizona. Remote viewing was a way to receive energy messages from the nonlocal dimension where all thought and spiritual energy not rooted in time, space, or physical dimension remains. It is from this nonlocal dimension that all mediums receive their divine guidance and messages. In this nonlocal dimension is the God source and connection to all life. It is a belt of knowledge past, present, and future swirling through eternity from which we, as aspects of that divine source, derive the illusion of physical life.

The reality is that we are eternal beings of light or energy interconnected to each other and to all that is or has been. As eternal sources of energy, it is even possible to exist in this and other time experiences. Perhaps we are only pure thought and ultimately here to become more conscious citizens of the Universal Cosmos.

To be at one with one's own energy and to be in balance with the energy of others are true keys to the gateway of the divine.

❖

This Father's Day weekend, I ran into Timothy O'Brien at my office. We always enjoy talking and smiling. He is a passionate follower of Jesus and God and trying hard to conquer his own human weaknesses and rise to a higher connection with Spirit. He was so excited to tell me that he had viewed Gary Busey on television. Busey is an actor who had a near-death experience. Timothy told me Gary talked about being unable to look into the magnificent bright light and had felt such peace and love during that near-death experience that he was ready to give up his physical life, but spiritual beings told him that he had work to complete in this life.

It is years later from the writing of that story, and this weekend will be Father's Day weekend again. Last night, I watched a new pilot for a show on the TNT cable network entitled *Proof*, which is the story of a surgeon who is commissioned by a dying billionaire to find out the truth about dying and what lies beyond. She is hesitant to take on this mission and is repressing the memory of her own near-death experience when she almost drowned. During that event, she saw her teenage son, who had died the previous year. One would think that having that experience would be enough to make her want to follow through and learn more about the process of dying and transitioning into spiritual life, but fear of changing long-held beliefs shut her down and kept her suspended in animation, awaiting the next big jolt of truth or faith before she might be moved to awaken and seek the truth.

CHAPTER 31
It's a Small Word After All

Inaction breeds doubt and fear. Action breeds confidence
and courage. If you want to conquer fear, do not sit
home and think about it. Go out and get busy.
Dale Carnegie

I received a letter from my son, Gregg, today asking for help and participation in his campaign to raise awareness and funds for the Juvenile Diabetes Research Foundation, an organization deeply dedicated to improving the life of all affected with type 1 diabetes and ultimately committed to finding a cure.

In the letter, Gregg expressed the fact that 2009 had been a very special year for him. He had celebrated his first wedding anniversary, found out that he was having his first child, and had gotten his first dog, Trajan, a diabetic medical alert dog trained to alert him of dangerous, life-threatening low blood sugars.

September 4, 2009, also marked his first decade of being a diabetic. Like with any long-term relationship, upon reflecting on what those ten years meant for him, he realized he had used 36,500 finger sticks to test his blood sugar, had 10,950 shots to deliver insulin, and had absorbed 730,000 extra calories to combat the effects of low blood sugar. In other words, these facts help to explain why living with this disease can be so cruel and debilitating.

As Gregg's mom, I have watched him accept and work with the challenges of this condition. Gregg is always going forward with hope for helping others to learn how to live a successful life, as he is doing. He finds the joy in his own life while concentrating on turning this challenge into a positive channel for his own spiritual growth. I would not have wished this condition on Gregg or any child or loved one, but I hope that good does eventually come out of difficulty. I encourage surrendering to the challenge and struggle and reaching with a trusting arm towards that higher purpose at work. A parent whose child also has diabetes and was very angry about it once said to me, "My child will die."

Well, each of us will die, some of us sooner than others. I like to think about living and appreciating each day and am so grateful that Gregg embraced this concept to the best of his ability, trying to implement healing approaches into every facet of his daily life.

Gregg was recently asked to write an article for a foundation dealing with children's diseases. The title of his article was, "It's a Small Diabetic World After All." He told a story that I believe clearly shows divine intervention. The story reads as follows:

My Dominican Republic vacation started much like any other. As a diabetic, packing is always an adventure. This trip was no different. The alarm rang at 4:30 AM, and we frantically scrambled to make our 7 AM flight. Right before leaving the house, I packed my current vial of insulin, along with a brand-new bottle for backup. This would be more than enough to get me through six days.

We made it to the Dominican Republic albeit a day late, and ultimately a bottle of insulin short. Whenever I travel, and arrive at my final destination, I unpacked my supplies, and placed any insulin I have in the hotel room refrigerator. This time my backup bottle of insulin, the one still in the box, was Symin, rather than my prescribed brand of Humalog. This was okay since this was only my backup bottle, and I still had my open vial with me. I thought it best to do an inventory.

It's funny, we diabetics tend to have a knack for eyeing measurements such as that plate looks like 40 grams of carbs, or that pizza requires five units. In this case, my first thought was that bottle has about four days of insulin at best. So, I was short on insulin, but not a problem, since this particular all-inclusive resort had a 24-hour on-call doctor and clinic. I should have read the fine print because, apparently, all-inclusive does not include insulin. Dr. Resort listened to my story and nearly laughed, but kindly responded, "I don't know, man, this is not easy to find." He told me he would make a few calls, and to check back the following day. I've listened, I checked in, no insulin, and no chance. Now, three days of insulin, and five days of vacation to go.

The following day, Lea and I passed a young boy at the pool. I noticed out of the corner of my eye what appeared to be a set, as well as a tan line, from another one. My wife convinced me that I needed to ask for help. Turns out young Nicholas was fourteen, diabetic, Danish, and leaving two days before us. His parents graciously offered to leave me with whatever insulin they had the day they were leaving, which turned out to be a nearly full bottle of Novalog. I felt like I found a needle in a haystack. What are the chances?

As September 4, 2009 would mark my ten-year anniversary with diabetes, and each and every day I learn something new, this trip was a reminder that the world is a small place, and diabetes is not exclusive to one country or region. Lucky for me that the same insulin I need to survive in San Francisco is what young Nicholas uses, but what seems so accessible for us is not so easily obtainable for others. Try and remember that for each shot we take somebody somewhere is missing out on theirs. That's why I work for a cure. That's why I will not stop until we have one.

❖

This next story represents our passage through time and space, through life and death, through love and the cycles of life, and to our evolving eternal life stories. Whether young or old, whether in a joyful or saddened time of our journey, we are continually being reminded by the Universal Force of Life that we are interconnected and entwined in each other's states of emotion and constantly offered opportunities for remembering the common themes that filter through our thoughts, actions, behaviors, and ultimate choices. No matter how small or large, our experiences are the vehicles for our transformation, refinement, and for acceptance of our life plan, and they assist our movement from this state of purely physical life awareness and the ordinary circumstances of our daily existence to change, refine, and transform so we may eventually bring a more empowered, refined version of our spirit back home to Eternal Life.

It was at hospice today that a story unfolded that showed me how kindness is a virtue and an element of all lives, all ages, and all dimensions. I entered a room where a pale, elderly woman was in a state, not quite asleep and not quite awake. Introducing myself, I asked if she would like me to sit with her. She did not respond, yet I knew her name was Eve.

As I sat quietly by her side, I noticed she was very thin, fragile like a china doll, and was close to 100 years old, as the nurse who was on duty had told me. Suddenly, she turned to me with open eyes and cried out, telling me that she was blind. I realized she was frightened, perhaps confused, and asked her if she would like me to put on a musical CD by Botticelli. We could listen to the heavenly music together. I told her my mother used to think he sang like an angel and then put on the music, sitting down in the chair by her side. The music had been on for a short time, and Eve started to cry again and got very agitated. I held her hand and asked what was wrong. She said she didn't hear me and thought I had left. I told her I could stay for a while and she had many kind people taking care of her.

As I closed my eyes, in my inner vision, I sensed a childlike form flit by me, and it felt like a sister she used to play hide-and-seek with. I asked her if she had a sister, and she told me her sister had died long ago. I asked if she remembered the fun they had together, and she laughed and was tickled to think of a sister she had loved and the times they had shared. As we sat together, I sent peaceful thoughts her way and the hope that when she was ready, her sister would take her hand and walk with her into her new life. At the end of the music, I asked her how she liked it, and she responded, "I love it." I believe she might have been responding more to another human being touching her hand with loving energy than to just the music, though the music, which was so beautiful, may have touched her soul. Upon leaving, I told her I would think of her and wish for her safety and peaceful rest, as she would not ever be alone.

The past is but the beginning of a beginning, and all that
is and has been is but the twilight of the dawn.
H.G. Wells

Epilogue

November 7, 2016

Today, as the 17th anniversary of my mother's death, is also a day of mixed emotions for me, with sadness sitting alongside gratitude. It is also the day before the people of our nation vote to elect our 45th president of the United States. I have always thought that the day of a person's death is the beginning of a new life in Spirit beyond the physical world. All new life offers opportunities for learning and for experiencing ways to communicate ideas, refine relationships, develop skills and values, and move us towards incorporating greater compassion and love within. My concerns, like the concerns of so many ordinary citizens of our country, are focused on the many problems facing the nation and on the necessary changes that must be made in our national and international policies.

The two candidates couldn't be more different nor represent such different visions for the future direction of the country and world. The unrest and openly angry attitudes of the populace created by the huge divide between the Democrats and Republicans and policies of past administrations that have been intent on achieving globalization, often at the expense of our democratic and national interests, has never been more palpable. In light of these problems and because George Washington stories have appeared throughout this book, I felt compelled to meditate and see if the soul essence, personality, and life force of our first president would come through in meditation and if he would answer a few questions. I had been successful when attempting to reach my sister who had passed recently, and though I usually only do a reading when asked by a client, I have been told over the years by other mediums that I can connect with any historical figure if I need further information about any subject. In the past, I was reluctant to intrude on another soul whom I never knew in life and who was not seeking to find me or bring a message to their relatives or friends. However, I had been having dreams of Mr. Washington for quite some time. Then when Master Ryuho Okawa, founder of Happy Science, a spiritual foundation in Japan, and a guest on my radio show, *Healing from Within*, had only days ago sent me his book entitled *Spiritual Interview with George Washington*. I put aside his book temporarily, deciding to read it after doing my own intuitive reading with President Washington. Like so many of us, I wanted to understand what I and others could do to help our nation in this time of turmoil and unhappiness.

I began the reading the way I normally do, by sitting in my office with the lights turned down and with soft music playing in the background. I centered myself, and then I simply asked President Washington if he would be so kind as to join me.

I felt the energy shift and flow around my shoulders and had an impression of a large triangular hat on George Washington's head and a second inverted triangle on balanced shoulders. It was later pointed out to me that the image I saw was the sign of the Freemasons, a group that Washington and the Founding Fathers were members of.

Then I sensed the president sitting at a large mahogany desk and writing as he relayed to me, "Know it was important to perform acts of kindness in the world and ensure the decency of future generations."

He went on to share, "We took time to make this nation come into existence, and the pain for accomplishing this was sorely felt by the women who watched war and suffering.

"With an open heart, we proudly flew the flag then, and it must still fly bravely today—the values are the same 200 years later. It is only love for this nation and the hardships of its birth that can help Americans go forward. Remember who you are in tradition and in freedom for *all*."

As I saw boots being pulled on, I sensed his thought, "Put on your boots and march alongside with the souls of the past, for the truth of freedom has not changed. It has only been forgotten by some."

I saw in my inner vision four or five geometric shapes of light floating overhead and sensed, "It's like holding moonbeams in your hand or merging with light that helps you flow through life and beyond in a continuing group of souls that delights and enlightens the world." Then I thought of the song "Catch a Falling Star," which reminded me that no matter how challenging life is or how many raindrops or tears may fall, hope will carry us along. Hope is necessary.

I asked the president why he came into my dreams and if I knew him before this time and place.

In response, I was shown a maypole with ribbons flowing from the top of the pole. I immediately remembered when I was in third grade, I performed in a school dance program around a maypole, joining with my classmates and friends. I immediately sensed this thought from President Washington, "Like the maypole dance of lovers, sons and daughters, families, centuries of souls, generation after generation, on following righteous and enduring traditions—the joy is eternally the same. Dance with love. It is the way to peace for you and our troubled nation." After the reading, wanting to know more about the maypole dance tradition, I went to Google and found the following information: "Maypole dancing is a form of folk dance from western Europe especially England, Northern Spain, Finland, Sweden, Portugal, and Germany."

President Washington ended with, "Like the sands of time returning to the beginning to start again. Patience and perseverance are the way."

Over the years of engaging in readings, I have discovered that my first and last message always go together, offering a clearer way to see what Spirit considers most important for us to remember. In hearing President Washington's words where he describes his connection to the Freemasons' search for truth and mystery in life, including scientific truths and philosophic concepts, the first and last messages received showed me his yearning as an ethical and moral leader to ensure that kindness and decency, the legacy of his generation, would remain for our citizens and the world forever. In the last message, by suggesting the need for patience and perseverance, regardless of corruption and misguided behavior, he wished the values of our spiritual ancestors to return and flourish. Our spiritual guides never tell us what to do, allowing us free will to rediscover or learn anew what we need in present situations and to value what is good. If we sense within our deepest memories the lives of past ancestors and past generations, retaining the best of what was won through their struggles and also their sacrifices, we will provide positive Universal energy that resonates with happiness and brings healing to our world.

During this reading, the music on my CD player began to skip and repeat in a very strong, uncomfortable manner, and I was unable during that interference to continue channeling George Washington's stream of thoughts.

Sometimes with powerful dynamic energies of evolved souls, which I believe President Washington to be, for he sacrificed so much to lead our people to freedom, that interplay of energies does happen. The feelings I experienced during this reading brought me such joy, almost bringing me to tears. I felt and knew in my heart the great love this particular soul has for life, his country, the world, and also for me as he shared his words so tenderly with me.

November 8, 2016

It is the day after the election. I stayed up until three o'clock in the morning to hear the final results and was thankful to hear that across our great nation, the citizens had rallied to the call of Donald Trump for change or simply a return to our basic values, growth, and preservation of our original, traditional constitutional laws, honoring a nation that was founded on the blood and sacrifices of patriots to ensure freedom for all religions, socio-economic factions, racial groups, immigrants, and intellectual or diverse thinkers. Nowhere in the world do we have a mixture of people as diverse and yet as unified as in the United States of America. No matter what differences we seem to have now, the changes that will come from these disruptive times may make us finally appreciate the greatness of our American democracy. Those who are less than satisfied with American democracy, which is always evolving, are free to find another part of the world to live, but they usually choose not to. And we as a Spiritual nation under God are the holders of light and truth for our populace and the world. That is why in the past we have been afforded great success and prosperity. Donald Trump is the 45th President of the United States, and like our first president, George Washington, his election comes out of troubled and turbulent events in the world and at home. President Trump tells us to rely on him and he will work for the people, and I believe that he will do just that. President Trump will help our declining nation to once again be responsible in our relationships with many nations that rely on our leadership and stability.

Our democracy was designed to afford us the freedom to have our own beliefs and express them without fear of retribution. That makes us unique as a nation. We will not allow ourselves to be intimidated by political dissent or other nations that threaten this reality. Our personal intuitive power within helps us, if we are truly in alignment with the original values of this nation and Spirit, to know a greater comprehensive truth and to consciously select leaders and policies that will enhance our growth and our success in all areas of life. In the past as a nation and individually, there have been many problems and issues, including slavery and mistreatment of Native Americans, as well as lack of understanding for many religious and cultural groups. Even though we have made mistakes and even though one person's truth may not be another person's truth, we have tried to remain open to new possibilities for continued improvement. The United States has welcomed immigrants from every country in the world in our hopes of achieving fairness and the American dream at the same time. While we as a nation and as humans can never be perfect, we can continue to strive for unity and oneness over time.

Well, we can certainly conclude from this information shared by the spirit of President George Washington that our nation, indeed our world, has always struggled and it has never been any different. There has always been friction, war, poverty, and self-serving individuals. War brings tragedy; separation between religions, political groups, and nations; and a disintegration of peace, beauty, progress, and the fullness or potential for our best human efforts. Without considering the needs of all, we will disavow generations of many righteous people who believed in our democracy and who fought for laws providing justice for *all*.

It is in this tradition, and for all the gains we have made over the centuries, that we must remember the goals of our Founding Fathers. We must not be so eager to forget our basic American values and our love of freedom. We must remember all the hard work of so many souls that led to the many accomplishments that preserve and honor the efforts of our citizens.

There is a foundation of goodness that resides in the American people, and we have shared our goodness with so many countries worldwide in the hopes that they can achieve their own liberation and perhaps democracy. It is our continuing responsibility and our destiny to show the world that the democracy of our Founding Fathers is still the most well-thought-out and best blueprint for bringing wisdom through action into the world.

I truly hope that other nations join the enlightened action that will be taken by our new president to ensure peace and love for life while retaining the best of our ideologies and adding innovative ideas and practices so that we are always moving forward as "One Nation Under God."

About the Author

In 1993, Sheryl had a dream and her grandfather, in Spirit, whispered to her, "You have to write something for your Father." The next morning Sheryl received a phone call from her mother announcing her father had passed, prompting her to write her father's eulogy. Unable to forget the energy of that connection to her grandfather in spirit, Sheryl began a journey of self-investigation trying to understand the feelings of her childhood where she saw faces in the window at night and felt touches on her arms while trying to fall asleep. Always knowing there was a bigger life force, she was not raised to believe in an afterlife. This dream, she learned in days to come, was a "spiritual visitation" and Sheryl has learned to open up to the energetic forces of Universal Source and has developed her innate healing connection to healing energy and to receiving messages from the Divine.

Sheryl Glick is the author of *Life is No Coincidence: The Life and Afterlife Connection* and The Living *Spirit: Answers for Healing and Infinite Love* and *A New Life Awaits: Spirit Guided Insights to Support Global Awakening* which completes the trilogy that Sheryl's grandfather and other messengers along the way told her she was required to accomplish. It was a contract made to Spirit to share the truth of our human and Divine being.

Sheryl is the host of Healing From Within which can be heard on www.sherylglick.com, www.webtalkradio.net, www.dreamvisions7radio.com. Sheryl and her accomplished guests explore the many facets of universal energy healing and the aligning of our physical and inner being for a complete, healthy, and dynamic human experience and encourages the most loving ways for us to reach out to each other as we develop into more civilized and conscientious human beings.

In dreams, coincidences, synchronistic happenings, Sheryl has discovered that life is but a series of miracles and divine intervention and we are never alone.

For more information about **A New Life Awaits Spirit Guided Insights to Support Global Awakening**

visit www.sherylglick.com
516-528-1967
Sheryl@SherylGlick.com
www.sherylglick.com

Suggested Reading List

Adler, Luke. *Born to Heal.* Rochester, VT, Healer Press, 2016.

Ale, Guy Joseph. *Buddha and Einstein Walk Into a Bar.* Newburyport, MA, Weiser Books, 2018.

Anderson, Ruth. *Walking With Spirit.* Ithaca, NY, Sagehouse Press, 2018.

Atwater, P.M.H. *A Manual for Developing Humans.* New Hyde Park, NY, Rainbow Ridge Books, 2017.

Bauer, Blake D. *You Were Not Born to Suffer: Overcome Fear, Insecurity and Depression and Love Yourself Back to Happiness, Confidence and Peace,* Seattle, WA, CreateSpace, 2013.

Bogart, Greg. *Dreamwork in Holistic Psychotherapy of Depression.* London, UK, Karnac Books, 2009.

Boyle, Sherianna. *Choosing Love.* Avon, MA, Adams Media, 2015.

Brown, Shari Sharifi. *The Seven Commandments for Happiness and Prosperity.* New York, NY, 2017.

Brooks, Ray. *The Shadow That Seeks The Sun.* London, England, Watkins Publishing, 2018.

Burk, Larry. Kanavos, Kathleen O'Keefe. *Dreams That Can Save Your Life.* Scotland, UK., Findhorn Press, 2018.

Calleman, Carl Johan, Ph.D. *The Global Mind and the Rise of Civilization.* Rochester, VA, Bear and Company, 2016.

Cappannelli, George, and Cappannelli, Sedena C. *Do Not Go Quietly.* Lithia Springs, GA, World Tree Press, 2013.

Carter, Michael J.S, Rev. *God Consciousness.* Nashville, TN, Grave Distractions, 2015.

Christopher, David. *The Holy Universe.* Santa Rosa, CA, New Story Press, 2013.

Crenshaw, Tobin. *The Beautiful Lie*. Pasadena, CA, Bestseller Publishing, 2018.

Deir, Linda. *Guided*. San Bernadino, CA, Guided Press, 2014.

Eaton, Barry. *The Joy of Living*. Sydney, Australia, Rockpool Press, 2017.

Engle, Debra Landwehr. *Be the Light that You Are*. Charlottesville, VA, Hampton Roads Publishing Company, Inc, 2019.

Fallois, Isabelle Von. *The Power of Your Angels*. Scotland, UK, Findhorn Press, 2014.

Fievet, Paddy. *The Making of a Mystic*. San Diego, CA, McKinnon Publishing, 2014.

Flaherty, Lorraine. *Healing with Past Life Therapy*. Scotland, UK, Findhorn, 2013.

Fowler, Raymond E. *The Andreasson Affair*. Englewood Cliffs, NJ, Prentice-Hall, 2014.

Friedel, EZ M.D. *Marilyn's Red Diary*. India, Sand Shack LLC, 2013.

Gallenberger, Joseph. *Heaven is for Healing: A Soul's Journey After Suicide*. New Hyde Park, NY, 2017.

Greer, Carl. *Change Your Story, Change Your Life*. Scotland, UK, Findhorn Press, 2014.

Hall, Adam C. *The Earth Keeper*. Lumsden, New Zealand, Waterfront Digital, 2014.

New York, NY, TarcherPergiee, 2015. Print

Heyes, Doug. *The Touch: Healing Miracles and Methods*. Scotland, UK, Findhorn Press, 2016.

House, Richard M.D. *Between Now and When: How My Death Made My Life Worth Living*. Pompton Plains, NJ, New Page Books, 2015.

Howitt, David, Esq. *Heed Your Call*. New York, NY, Atria Books, 2014.

Hubbard, Barbara Marx. *The Evolutionary Testament of Co-Creation*. Los Angeles, CA, Muse Harbor, 2015.

Hunter, Allan G. *Gratitude and Beyond: Five Insights for a Fulfilled Life*. Scotland, UK, Findhorn Press, 2013.

Hunter, Brent N. *The Rainbow Bridge to Inner Peace and to World Peace.* Philadelphia, PA, BookBaby, 2014.

Jankel, Nick Seneca. *Switch On.* London, UK, Watkins, 2015.

Jones, Marie D., and Flaxman, Larry. *Mind Wars.* Pompton Plains, NJ, New Page, 2015.

Kagan, Annie. *The Afterlife of Billy Fingers.* Charlottesville, VA, Hampton Roads Publishing, 2013.

Mattingly, Annie. *The Afterlife Chronicles.* Newburyport, MA, Hampton Roads Publishing, 2017

Mardlin, Emma. *Out of Your Comfort Zone.* Scotland, UK, Findhorn Press, 2019.

Mardlin, Emma. *Mind Body Diabetes Type 1 and Type 2: A positive, powerful, and proven solution to stop diabetes once and for all..* Scotland, UK, Findhorn Press, 2016.

Martin, Barbara Y, Moraitis, Dimitri. *Communing with the Divine.* New York, NY, TarcherPerigee, 2014.

McQulillen, Joe. *My Search for Christopher on the Other Side.* Lisa Hagan Books. 2018

Muhl, Lars. *The Gate of Light.* London, England, Watkins Publishing, 2018.

Okawa, Ryuho Master. *Messages from Heaven.* New York, NY, IRH, 2015.

Okawa, Ryuho Master. *-Miraculous Ways to Conquer Cancer.* New York, NY, IRH, 2014.

Okawa, Ryuho Master. *-The Heart of Work.* New York, New York, IRH, 2016.

Peirce, Penney. *Leap of Perception.* New York, NY, Atria Books, 2013.

Peters, Ted. *UFOs--God's Chariots?* Atlanta, GA, John Knox, 1977. 2011.

Redfern, Nicholas. *Bloodline of the Gods.* Brompton, IN, New Page Books, 2015.

Redfern, Nicholas. *Weapons of the Gods.* Brompton, IN, New Page Books, 2016.

Rou, Monk Yun. *Mad Monk Manifesto.* Miami, FL, Mango Publishing, 2018.

Sauvage, Lester M.D. Little, Barbara Mulvey (co-author). *Opening Hearts*. Better Life Press, 2015.

Schuitmaker, Lisette. *The Childhood Conclusions*. Scotland, UK, Findhorn Press, 2017.

Sluyter, Dean. *Fear Less*. New York, NY, TarcherPerigee, 2018.

Solheim, Bruce Olav. *Timeless*. Scotts Valley, CA, CreateSpace Publishing, 2018.

Templeton, James. *I Used to Have Cancer*. New Hyde Park, NY, Square One Publishers, 2019.

Thurston, Mark. *Discovering Your Soul's Purpose*. New York, NY, TarcherPerigee, 2017.

Vallyon, Imre. *The Journey Within*. Hamilton, New Zealand, Sounding-Light, 2015.

Viljoen, Edward. *The Power of Meditation*. New York, NY, Tarcher Perigee, 2013.

Walsch, Tara Jenelle. *Soul Courage*. Faber, VA, Rainbow Ridge Books, 2015.

Weiner, Chaney. *Because This Is Your Life*. Lakeview, MA, Inspired Living Worldwide, 2015.

Woodard, TJ. *Conscious Being: Awakening to Your True Nature*. Bloomington, IN, Balboa, Press 2015.

www.ingramcontent.com/pod-product-compliance
Lightning Source LLC
Chambersburg PA
CBHW030823090426
42737CB00009B/843